SIMONE WEIL
AND
THE SUFFERING OF LOVE

SIMONE WEIL AND THE SUFFERING OF LOVE

Preface by
Robert Coles

ERIC O. SPRINGSTED

WIPF & STOCK · Eugene, Oregon

Wipf and Stock Publishers
199 W 8th Ave, Suite 3
Eugene, OR 97401

Simone Weil & The Suffering of Love
By Springsted, Eric O.
Copyright©1986 by Springsted, Eric O.
ISBN 13: 978-1-60899-094-8
Publication date 1/11/2010
Previously published by Cowley Publications, 1986

ACKNOWLEDGMENTS

I owe a great deal of thanks to a number of people who have made this book possible. Cynthia Shattuck, editor of Cowley Publications, has supported and encouraged this project for probably longer than either of us would like to remember. Diogenes Allen and various members of the American Weil Society have constantly challenged me to think and rethink a number of issues. Richard West of St. John's United Church of Christ in Chicago has given me much to think about in terms of some of the hard, concrete applications of Weil's understanding of affliction to life as many people have to live it. A friend who must remain unnamed has given me a great deal of information about Weil personally. Finally, I owe my greatest thanks to my wife and daughters, who certainly experienced their share of patient waiting during the time it took to prepare this book.

                                        Eric O. Springsted

PREFACE TO THE 2010 EDITION

When *Simone Weil and the Suffering of Love* was initially published in 1986, not many books on Weil had been published, especially in English, and those that were, were not always readily available. Most were introductions to her life and thought, combining biographical narrative with a survey of her chief ideas presented in a way that tended towards the itemized. In the areas of philosophical and theological analysis, there was first of all Miklos Vëto's *La Metaphysique religieuse de Simone Weil* (1971). It was available in French and some other languages, but not English. It was the first genuine philosophical examination of her thinking. Beyond that, three years earlier I had published my dissertation, *Christus Mediator: Platonic Mediation in the Thought of Simone Weil*. These two were pretty much the only books available at the time that gave a detailed philosophical and theological examination of Weil's thinking as a whole and how it held together.

So when *Simone Weil and the Suffering of Love* was first published, it was meant to provide a clear and somewhat systematic introduction to Weil's religious thinking; in doing so, it meant to take that thinking largely on its own merits, without reducing its strongest and most controversial aspects to outworkings of Weil's psychology. Weil's important understanding of love and suffering was an insight, not a veiled perverse biographical narrative. Thus this book meant to show what her central ideas were about suffering and love and God, and how they led into, interpenetrated, and drew together all the other aspects of Weil's thought. Weil was not a thinker who ever attempted anything like a system; she thought philosophical systems were largely poetry. But, still, her thought is highly integrated, even when it is also highly provocative and paradoxical. This book therefore meant to give both to the beginner and the scholar a sense of that cohesiveness, and of the challenge it offered to many of our ideas about the human and divine good, love, and suffering. It also meant to demonstrate, as *Christus Mediator* had before it, that Weil's religious thinking was firmly rooted in her understanding of Christ's cross.

The initial publication of this book, however, as time has told, was part of a happily and rapidly increasing number of books on Weil. In each year since then there have been a number of new books that have appeared on Weil. These have included some fine introductions and biographies, as well as detailed studies on various aspects of her thought—social, political, philosophical and religious. The updated select bibliography to this edition attests to what has been written during this time.

These many years later, the need for an introduction, given the number of good books that have since appeared on Weil, may therefore seem less pressing than it did in 1986. However, this still is one of a few books that does give a thorough and cohesive understanding of Weil's religious thought. It also has at its core an argument that needs to be taken seriously in thinking about Weil, namely, that her religious thinking, while owing much to Greek philosophy and other religions, has its nerve center in the historical cross. Weil, to be sure, thought the cross was of universal and cosmic impact, and wrote with this firm conviction in mind; but the universal always proceeded from the particular for her on this issue. In this respect, I believe that those who, like the great Hans Urs von Balthasar (in *Mysterium Paschale*), have suggested that for Weil the cross is the *symbol* of a religious universal, and that she subordinated it to a pre-Christian universal have turned things around. It is maintained here, on the contrary, that Weil took the concrete and historical cross most seriously and found its mediation of divine love the ground on which all other mediations of God to human thought and culture were subsequently grounded—including Greek geometry. This is what she meant when she quoted the *Apocalypse* to the effect that Christ was "the lamb slain from the foundation of the world." The concreteness of the cross is the historical root and center of God's love for the world, and Christ's actual, historical self emptying (*kenosis*) is the paradigm of divine goodness and love. This republication allows

Preface

that argument to be made available again. Moreover, the attempt of this book to be wide ranging in its treatment of Weil's numerous writings hopefully grounds that argument firmly in the text as it should be.

Most of all, though, in the end this is a book that is meant to help readers, whether novices or professional, understand Weil, and even more so to help the reader understand the mystery of the divine reality that Weil thought surrounds us and that gives us life, and it should be read in that light first of all.

There are, I suppose, any number of things that are said here in ways that I would put differently now. I have spent much time in recent years developing the ideas of the chapter "The Love of God in Daily Life," that makes what is said there sometimes appear to be more suggestive than finalized. Still, this book still firmly stands on its own. The one change of mind I have had, though, and that I do think should be noted here is the comment on page 6 that Weil "was probably a victim of *anorexia nervosa*." Whatever issues there may be concerning Weil's willfulness with respect to food, and there are many, I think that after Dr. Robert Coles's analysis of the situation, that this clinical designation does not accurately apply to her, and that the occasional attempts of some biographers to pin it on her, and then to develop an entire aetiology and pathology based on it are misguided.

CONTENTS

SIMONE WEIL
    OUTSIDER OR INSIDER?   1

FORCE   17

THE SUFFERING OF LOVE   37

THE WEIGHT OF LOVE   53

THE SACRIFICE OF LOVE   75

THE LOVE OF GOD IN DAILY LIFE   99

EPILOGUE   125

Notes   133

Bibliography   134

SIMONE WEIL
OUTSIDER OR INSIDER?

"The world needs saints who have genius, just as a plague-stricken town needs doctors. Where there is a need, there is an obligation."

Waiting for God

When Simone Weil died in a tuberculosis sanitarium in 1943 at the age of thirty-four, those who knew her could have expected her to be remembered in a number of ways. Simone de Beauvoir's memories of her as a student recall her as a brilliant intellectual whom others held in great awe, but who would weep at the news of a devastating earthquake on the other side of the globe. Weil was also the one who could make de Beauvoir feel like a "petty bourgeois" for putting philosophical questions ahead of the need to feed the masses. The unemployed workers of the town of Le Puy would have remembered her as the philosophy professor at the girl's lycée who led them in protest against the municipal authorities. Readers of left-wing journals would have remembered her for her trenchant social criticism. And the workers in three Paris factories, if they had known who she was, would have remembered her as the professor who worked alongside them for a year in order to come into contact with the object of her reflections on labor.

Simone Weil has been remembered for all these things. But now there is something for which she is particularly known that almost nobody suspected in 1943; that is, the profundity of her religious thought. Although Weil had written to her confidante, Father Perrin, about three intense mystical experiences that bound her heart unalterably to Christ, and although she almost daily experienced his mystical presence while praying the Lord's Prayer in Greek, virtually none of this was known until after her death. At that time a small book was published, *Gravity and Grace*, which contained aphorisms culled from her voluminous notebooks. The spiritual depth was immediately apparent, but it came as a surprise. Her brother André, a prominent mathematician, recalls that once he challenged her on her interpretation of Plato as a true mystic; Weil replied that not everyone who is a mystic talks about it openly. Little did André Weil suspect at the time the personal reference.

Forty years later, however, it is her religious thought for which Weil is best known, although the impact of her political and social thought has not diminished in importance. That religious thought is at the same time traditional and contemporary, Christian and universal. She is traditional in that she holds steadfastly to the historic doctrines of the Trinity, of creation from nothing, and of the incarnation of Christ and his redemptive death. She holds unabashedly to a high view of transcendence, and even reintroduces the ancient and medieval view of the world as a hierarchy of superimposed levels with sacramental meaning for those who are able to discern them. But these traditional views reflect also the understanding Weil gained from reading and borrowing from non-Christian sources such as Hinduism, Buddhism, and the ancient Greeks, especially Plato. In fact, as far as we can tell, a great deal of the structure of her thought, even at the places where it is materially most traditional, is owed to these sources and not to any deep knowledge of classical Christian thinkers. If she is Augustinian (and she is), it is not because she was well-read in Augustine, but rather because of a Platonic Christianity they held in common.

Yet at the same time Weil's thinking is contemporary. Refusing the evolutionary schemes so popular in the French philosophy of her day (such as Bergson) as well as in much of our own, she accepted the verdict of modern science that has forbidden us to speak of a purpose in the workings of nature. Like Camus and Sartre, she saw the world of nature as alien and often unfriendly to human purposes. Yet, unlike them, Weil did not see this cosmic alienation as the occasion for a heroic stance. Rather, the cold fact is something to be accepted, even if it strikes to the root of cherished views we hold about ourselves as persons, and contemplated in all its harsh purity as a part of the higher truth and beauty to which, by grace, we have access.

At first blush, all these elements within Weil's thought, while dazzling and admirable, appear as if they could only be held together by the most blatant form of syncretism. Yet Weil holds them together coherently with her doctrine of mediation. She argues that the creation of the world is accomplished by a "crucifixion" of God, perfected in the historic cross, which allows everything within creation to be related to every other thing through a mediating relation to God. We can as spiritual creatures then have access to the power of that mediation if we are willing to accept the crucifixion both intellectually *and* physically—if it should come to that. It is on condition of that acceptance that we can understand the harmony of the world, which includes all its parts— our personal and social being, our past and future, the unbending mathematical laws of nature, and all our needs for purpose and good—as existing within God's love.

If what Weil is saying has any truth, then she is well worth listening to as we struggle to integrate our past with the problems posed by our present, and our narrow concerns with our more universal problems. In that case she might very well be one of those "saints of genius" of whom she herself writes,

> Today it is not nearly enough to be a saint, but we must have the saintliness demanded by the present moment, a new saintliness itself without precedent. . . . The world needs saints who have genius, just as a plague-stricken town needs doctors. Where there is a need, there is an obligation. (WG, 99)

Despite this "need," however, when the world looks at Weil it often asks for a second opinion. Admittedly she was brilliant, and she loved both God and neighbor intensely. But on anybody's account Weil was no "philosophical Mother Theresa of the factories." There are difficulties both with her person and her thought, and a side to her that is rather more off-putting than enlightening.

We are troubled by Weil's life, and by some of the ideas that have sprung from it, in a number of very particular ways. Religiously she often appears quite heterodox, even to the point of gnosticism in the popular sense of that term—at times her emphasis seems entirely on the spiritual at the expense of the physical. Although claiming to be a Roman Catholic in sympathy and spirit, she steadfastly refused to be baptized until upon her death bed on the grounds she had not been commanded by God, and because she felt that entering the Church would exclude her from solidarity with those outside the Church, especially those of genuine spirituality. Additionally, there were large portions of the Old Testament she detested and she came close to Marcionism in asserting that the God of the New Testament could not have commanded certain acts described in the Old. In her attempts to see the light of the cross in all cultures and all parts of history, Weil expressed views on at least one occasion that seemed to accept other incarnations of God besides Jesus, such as the nine incarnations of Vishnu in Hinduism. Ironically, this denies her own emphasis on the unique act of the cross.

We may also have problems with her as an individual, particularly in the way she apparently viewed herself. Weil felt little kinship with Judaism, the religion of her birth, and in at least one unpublished manuscript seems to accept popularly-held views discriminatory to Jews. She had little interest in her own sexual identity and often attempted to be as man-like (or at least as unwomanly) as possible. As a joke, she would even occasionally sign letters to her parents as "your dutiful son." In the second place Weil was probably a victim of *anorexia nervosa*; this would partially explain the strict asceticism of her life and her almost blind lack of self-concern for her own person. Her attitude seems to indicate a spirit of self-immolation; her death, which occurred because of a refusal, and probably an inability, to eat while she was suffering from tuberculosis, seems to confirm this. All these facts taken together can easily lead to charges of self-hatred, suggesting an inhuman and fanatic quality about her that does not endear her to those to whom she is supposed to speak so eloquently. Her suffering seems foolish and misplaced.

When we read Weil's own writings on suffering carefully, however, it is our own scepticism that seems misplaced. We begin to suspect that a psychological reductionism will not do these writings justice any more than it would do justice to the works of

Augustine, Kierkegaard or Dostoevsky. We are then left in a quandary and ask, "How are all these things to be taken?"

In thinking about Weil, there are three factors that need to be brought into play: first, her ideas, insights, and critiques, which are the result of hard thought; then her personal reasons for acting as she did; finally, the circumstances over which she had no control—perhaps she was not even conscious of them. All three factors contribute to each other, and if the first is what ultimately matters to us as her readers, it is necessary to realize that those ideas and insights did not simply and easily proceed from the philosopher's syllogism. They are, certainly, the result of intelligence and awareness, but they are also the product of Weil having been, in Diogenes Allen's phrase, an "outsider." She was an outsider partly by choice, but sometimes she had no choice. Paradoxically, it is because she was an outsider, and still remains one, that she has so much to offer to those of us who are not.

An illustration of Weil's ideas, choices, and circumstances is found in her relation to the institutional Church. By way of a thought-out position she leaves a trenchant criticism of the Church—which, she admits, is divinely instituted and a "steward of the sacraments and guardian of the sacred texts." (GG, 72) But it is also a social institution, and as such belongs, as all such institutions do, to the Prince of this world. Mixed in with the Church's truth is a more dangerous aspect of the Church—the warm group feeling of belonging that is elevated to a kind of ersatz divinity. This is dangerous not just because it allows for a double standard, which is always ugly, but because it allows the institution to think that it is self-sufficient. As a consequence the Church keeps out as much light as it lets in, particularly in regard to the illumination that might be gained from so-called secular or pagan sources. The society of the Church easily blinds us to more universal service and ideals, and as a result we betray those causes to which we merely pay lip-service. Pointing to saints who approved the Crusades, Weil writes:

> If I think that on this point I can see more clearly than they did, I who am so far below them, I must admit

> that in this matter they were blinded by something
> very powerful. This something was the Church seen as
> a social structure. (WG, 53)

This is a criticism to which the Church needs to listen carefully whenever it attempts to divide the world into "we" and "they."

But Weil did not think that because of the social nature of the Church everybody ought to abandon it, and seek truth on their own; the Church is still the steward of the sacraments and guardian of the sacred texts. Yet she herself deliberately chose to remain outside until her death, and the reason she gives to Father Perrin in her letters is that to remain outside is a personal vocation for her and a matter of obedience to Christ. The Church, she says, should contain all vocations; ideally it does, but in fact this is not the case. When Weil saw the Church's deliberate exclusion through anathema of so many things she regarded as precious to God and from which she had gained inspiration, she felt it would be a betrayal of grace to renounce those things through entering the Church. Weil was not unalterably opposed to joining the Church, but she feared the constraints it might put on her work. She also feared she might be required to renounce all the heterodox sources of inspiration which she found so valuable. This for Weil was a personal reason, and not one of general principle. Its personal nature is reflected in the fact that Weil goes so far as to say that "if circumstances make intellectual work definitively and totally impossible for me," there might be no objection to be baptized. (WG, 86) When a friend with whom she had discussed baptism came to her shortly before her death and asked if she was ready to be baptized, Weil, surely knowing her work was at an end, could say: "Yes."[1]

There was one more barrier to Weil's joining to the Church, and that is one over which she had no control. She was neither born into nor brought up within the Church. In this sense, she did not elect to go outside the Church; she chose to stay there. It is important to understand this fact. Weil was Jewish, although her family did not practice Judaism nor did Weil herself have any sympathies with it. Nevertheless she was associated with Jews by others and constantly reminded of it by people on the street, by the anti-Jewish laws of Vichy France, and by those to whom she applied to be parachuted into occupied France during the war. Jews, like other minority groups, have never fared particularly well with the Church. In this regard Weil's outlook could not have helped being influenced by criticisms of the Church from the perspective of outsiders, and shaped as well by what is a strong anti-clerical feeling in France. In such cases the outsider minority group can often see the dominant group more clearly than the dominant group can see itself, and here Weil in criticizing the Church and choosing to remain outside of it is doing so with a well-informed perspective.

Most people, of course, are a combination of well-thought-out ideas, personal choices and accidental circumstances; in this, Weil is not unique. But a major clue to understanding her can be found in the way that these three factors operated in her life, for they have a definite thrust of direction. That thrust is always tending towards a vision that is pure and universal, even if it originally began in personal circumstances and was enhanced by personal decision. So when Weil writes on topics such as the Church or injustice or suffering, what she wants to convince people of is what the Church ought to be and what injustice and suffering really are. She does not want us to be sympathetic to her circumstances and to believe in her choices; each of us has circumstances and choices sufficient for ourselves. What she writes about is something all of us should see.

This thrust towards the pure and universal is something that gives Weil's thought its luminous character. When, for example, she criticizes the Church, her criticism is meaningful because it is not the glib complaint of the uncommitted and uninvolved. It has authority because she is involved and committed to the ideal. Her writings on suffering have a similar flavor, for they do not bemoan our injuries; rather, they seek to describe what those injuries really are and to see how there can still be goodness and life beyond injury.

If we can see this thrust, we can also see that there is a side to Weil that is both admirable and courageous. She did not content herself in her actions with a limited perspective. She sought to act on the ideals she had uncovered, even if this meant harm to herself. It is in this regard that Maurice Schumann, a close friend of Weil's in the Free French and now a member of the French Academy, has called Weil's death one "born of her life." Although suffering from tuberculosis, a condition that before the discovery of penicillin was treated in part by forcing the patient to overeat, she refused to compromise her resolve to eat no more than the ration allowed to children in occupied France. Weil's life was based on living according to such ideals; she would rather have an honorable death than a compromised life.

The purity of life that Weil sought has also made her in an important sense an "insider," for she attempted to think out and live her life in complete obedience to God's will. The rest of us are the ones outside true spirituality as a result of our compromises in ideals. We have a great deal to learn about the "inside" of spiritual life from people such as Weil.

Yet, even granting this, Weil still paradoxically remains an outsider in other ways and always will remain so. The fact is that no individual life, save that of Christ himself, can have universal significance. Perhaps in our capacity for thought we come close to purity and universality, but as individual people we cannot escape our limited nature. In her writings, particularly in her later ones, Weil realizes this. She addresses the problem of how a limited being in this world can remain aware of these limitations and yet can still live in light of the eternal. In many ways, though, Weil did not succeed in realizing this paradox in her own life; instead, she continually tried to behave as if the ideal could actually be realized. At times this led to some rather humorous situations. We, for example, understand and appreciate her idea that workers should understand the laws of nature to which they are subject in their labors; we are somewhat astounded, however, to hear of her trying to teach a peasant girl in the vineyards Euclid and Sanskrit poetry.

Weil did often try to ignore her own situation and limitations. Certainly the fact that she was not born into the Church, in addition to the fact of her being a woman, gave her a perspective that "insiders" cannot have. Yet as often as not she ignored and even denied those aspects of herself in seeking the universal. In part, this may have been because she was seeking a purity of idea, and these things she regarded as constrictions on that search. Rather than trying to change the convention, she simply ignored the constriction. If women, for instance, were not allowed to do certain kinds of work, and she wanted to find out what that work was like, she ignored the convention directly. We hear of her persuading some Portuguese fishermen to take her on an expedition, although most would not allow a woman on the boat. She learned what she wanted, but was apparently unaware of the scandal that was created among the women in the village.

The difficulty that this sort of action causes is that it leads to a certain brutality toward the self; in attempting to live the ideal, Weil forced herself to suffer the repercussions when she defied convention, not only socially and physically, but psychologically as well. In this there is a kind of courage that we have already noted, but there is also a side of Weil's character that positively invited suffering. In a 1943 letter to Maurice Schumann she claims, "Life for me means nothing, and never has meant anything, really, except as a threshold to the revelation of truth." (SL, 178) With that thought in mind Weil was perfectly willing to increase and use that suffering to gain more truth, even though she recognized her willingness as perverse. She wanted to use her life as an experiment to capture the essence of suffering and of being outside. In this sense she wanted to suffer, and she begged Schumann to send her on a dangerous mission into occupied France, saying,

> I have the inner certainty that this truth, if it is ever granted to me, will only be revealed when I myself am physically in affliction.... I am afraid it may not happen. (SL 173)

And so we are divided in our feelings about her. On the one hand, Weil is for us the great insider. She was a woman of courage, ideals and clear insight. Yet we cannot romanticize the fact because, on the other hand, she always remains outside much of our common life. But the difficult side of Weil need not finally dissuade us from listening to her, any more than we need be dissuaded from crossing a bridge that was originally constructed because someone took a big risk and threw up a footbridge between two sides of a gorge. It is because the first bridge was built, dangerous as it may have been, that the two sides were successfully joined and a stronger and safer bridge put in place that others who are more careful may cross. Weil's problematic nature may here be the only way the rest of us can learn to cross to the other side.

There is a similarity here between Weil and the German poet, Rainer Maria Rilke. All his life Rilke suffered from terrible depressions. When his friend, Lou Andreas-Salomé, offered to ask Sigmund Freud to analyze Rilke and relieve him of his depression, however, he refused on the grounds that health would destroy his poetic vision. We do not have to suffer as Rilke did to understand and appreciate what Rilke wrote, and we do not have to recreate Weil's sufferings in our own life to appreciate her vision. But we do have to take seriously the fact that the vision was gained by suffering and that its truth cannot be divorced from suffering.

Weil was physically unhealthy, a victim of migraine headaches all her life. At points in her life she may have been psychologically unhealthy as well, but as Susan Sontag comments on her and other "unhealthy" writers: "Their unhealthiness is their soundness and is what carries conviction."[2] Weil was willing to suffer as an outsider in order to gain her views. We do not take those views seriously if we cease to see the pain by which they had to be achieved.

Sontag, however, goes on to say that she does not believe that more than a handful of those who read Weil actually share her ideas, nor that it is necessary to do so, except in a piecemeal way. Yet this is to dissolve the hard paradox that Simone Weil presents. The fact that Weil is valuable to us is not just because she is more serious about these matters that we are; also of value to us is the way she thinks about the problems of spirituality and the conclusions she reaches.

When reading Weil one often gets the feeling she is writing from the viewpoint of God himself, particularly when she is invoking Plato as she often does. However a more careful reading reveals that she is deliberately writing with a clear view of the limits of the human being who wants to find the eternal, but is separated from it by what amounts to a void. We encounter that void when we seek an absolute good, the only thing that will fully satisfy us, and discover that our purposes and our hunger will never be satisfied in this world. While we remain disappointed, we still cannot go beyond the limitations of our earthly existence. But, Weil continues, there is also a mystery to existence that transcends those limits; by desire and grace, the soul can be touched by God himself. Given this contact with the divine, she believed, an incarnation of divine love is possible and thus a life of faith in which divine light might infuse all the thoughts and actions of human beings. It is here that Simone Weil does indeed have something true and lasting to say.

Weil gained these thoughts about the divine love by paying close attention to suffering, both in herself and in others. This attention to suffering is something that threads itself throughout her thought, even when that thought is at its most metaphysical and abstract. Yet her thinking is not ultimately morbid, for in accepting and thinking through the fact of suffering she finds joy. For her the way to that joy, however, must always consider suffering. Joy that cannot permeate suffering is only transitory. It is for that reason that in talking about Weil's thinking we must begin with her work on suffering, both in her writing and in her life.

FORCE

"Such is the nature of force. Its power to transform a man into a thing is double and cuts both ways; it petrifies differently, but equally, the souls of those who suffer it and of those who wield it."

"The *Iliad*: Poem of Force"

It was a principle of Thomas Aquinas' that one ought never to weaken one truth in order to strengthen another truth. Yet it is a tendency of individuals, and even whole ages, to be one-sided. If the ancient and medieval thinkers saw humans as creatures with souls and therefore, so it seemed to them, as creatures a little less than God, they did not fully recognize that such creatures are also to a large degree the products of a social and physical environment not directly related to spiritual forces. By contrast we moderns, who do not see scientific laws as purposeful, and who realize that material factors determine us to a greater extent than even we are comfortable with, have failed to recognize spirituality as something vitally important in human life and thought.

Simone Weil understood the modern view well. In her early political writings on Marx and in philosophical essays and her lectures on philosophy, she was unrelenting in her investigation of the degree to which we are only the subjects of external influences. In fact, she criticizes Marx for only having gone half-way in this regard. But Weil was never satisfied with that sort of investigation because it could not give a full account of ourselves, and she comments in an ironical tone that behaviorism is the best explanation of human nature—provided one doesn't believe it. We should not believe it because there is something in us that answers only to a reality that transcends the created world.

That quality about us helped Weil perceive that the modern tendency of material reductionism is more than the intellectual error of suppressing one truth for the sake of another. Reductionism also commits the moral error of taking what is sacred in humans and subordinating it to things that are less than perfectly good. There is a sanctity to human life, Weil thought, not derived from a "spark" of the divine at the center of our being, but rather because "at the center of the human heart, is the longing for an absolute good, a longing which is always there and is never appeased by any object in this world." (SE, 219) Corresponding to this longing is a divine reality outside space and time; that reality is the "sole foundation of good." Whenever we allow ourselves to be satisfied by anything less than that reality, and feed others with anything less, we are guilty of giving stones to hungry souls rather than bread. We are also guilty of a kind of idolatry by making the creature stand in the place of the creator.

The moral error is not without its effect, either, for when we bury and subordinate that longing for absolute good our lives become completely determined by circumstances, even in the realm of spirituality. We think we are self-sufficient and govern our own wills and the world around us. The belief is easily held if we think that all our hopes are within our limited grasp. This conviction that we can provide for our own good can have two disastrous consequences; namely, even in our most momentous affairs we proceed without any sense of what is really and ultimately good, and consequently when our expectations are disappointed by what the world gives, such as when we are made to suffer, we have nowhere to turn to find purpose in our lives. This last consequence is particularly evident in the extreme case of suffering that Weil called affliction. Tragically, each consequence is partner to the other.

The truth that modern thought has recognized is the great influence of the material world on so much of who we are. That influence is not evil, but it is troublesome when it is the only influence we can see and understand. If we cannot discern any other influence, we easily overestimate the importance of the effect the material world has on us. When we do so we can allow ourselves to be dominated by the material world even in our innermost being. The problem is not a modern problem as such, but it has a particular urgency now that our means of control over nature and society have become so subtle and powerful. It is in her 1939 essay, "The *Iliad*: Poem of Force," that Weil describes this influence and domination most powerfully. The essay is particularly important for us because there Weil does not attempt to come to a scholar's critique of Homer's poem about the Trojan War; rather, what she presents is an understanding of the soul which has been dominated by force and hence is most vulnerable to affliction. The essay is an understanding of the world and our place within it without reference to anything beyond the world of nature. In this sense it is the lesson we *ought* to learn from the Trojan War, and is a lesson about our relations in the world of nature. These relations only appear larger in the case of war.

The key to the lesson on the *Iliad*, Weil contends, lies in understanding that the true hero of that poem is not Achilles, Agamemnon, Hector and any other character. The hero is force. The force of which Weil speaks is not only coercion and compulsion, but also prestige; all of these things, she says, have their roots in the actions and reactions of brute matter. It is force alone, and thus matter, she says, that ultimately determines the thoughts and actions of the men and women of the Trojan War. By analogy, Weil bids us see the same quality in our relations in areas of human life other than war, and this despite our belief that we direct our own destinies.

Force can reduce us to little more than inanimate matter. This is true in the most literal sense, of course, when through the exercise of force a warrior is killed and reduced to a corpse. But, Weil goes on to observe, force can reduce human beings to little more than matter even while they are still breathing. A feature of being human is our power to exert pressure on the world and, in turn, resist it when it is turned on us; it is this ability that allows us to act and interact in the physical world. But in situations such as the *Iliad* describes, when the warrior is disarmed and waiting for the sword to strike and end his life, a human being can no longer exercise or resist force. The victim in such cases exercises no more influence on his assailant than does a stone that is kicked out of the way.

The force that people exercise is at its root nothing but physical force. It originates in nature and is part of nature's forces. We have always understood that physical force can destroy us, which is why we try to be careful in its exercise. Weil is concerned to show us that not only can force destroy us physically, it can also destroy psychically—it can destroy all inner life without killing. This is true not only in the case of the warrior about to be slain, it is also true in the case of slaves and of everyone who must, for whatever reason, obey the wills of others. Weil comments, "There is no difference between throwing a stone to get rid of a troublesome dog and saying to a slave: Chase that dog away." (WG, 142) To the person who exercises great force the stone and the very weak person are equivalent, because they both must do the bidding of the one who can forcefully manipulate them. Like the stone, the victim of force does not have to be consulted in the matter. Such a victim is not even allowed to experience misery. "One cannot lose more than the slave loses, he loses all inner life. He only retrieves a little if there should arise an opportunity to change his destiny." (IC, 30)

This much we might have expected, for we all fear physical force and are aware to some degree of what it can do to us if it is ever turned on us in any great magnitude. But why is the weak person so very weak in the face of the powerful, and why is the slave so helpless? It is certainly not usually the case that the slave is physically weaker than his master, or has been beaten into submission. Entire oppressed peoples, such as in South Africa, actually outnumber their dominators considerably. Weil herself notes that "the strong man is never absolutely strong, nor the weak man absolutely weak...." (IC, 34) The answer is that force is rarely so crude as to be limited to strength of arm. Rather, it appears in human relations under the more potent form of prestige.

Weil was at pains throughout all her works to show the great extent to which our personalities are simply the play of random forces. Personality, for Weil, is simply the accidental possession of certain innate or acquired features such as looks, talents, family influences, and so forth. It may also depend on the possession of certain external things, such as money. By themselves, these things are of little consequence; in relation to other people, however, who have been taught and believe that blonde hair, charisma, and the Rockefeller family name are prestigious, then looks, charisma, and family name become potent forces within a society. We can get things easily from other people by impressing them with the idea that we are important, that we have "clout," and the effect can be the same as if we were physically threatening. Because in the *Iliad* Agamemnon has the prestige of being king, Weil points out, he can take away Briseis from Achilles even though Achilles is the better warrior. By the same token Thersites, a mere soldier who offers advice to the council that is quite similar to Achilles' advice, is beaten and laughed at and told that he counts for nothing. In this regard then, despite the fact that she is never without power, the weak and oppressed person cannot help but feel that she is of a different species than the strong person. The strong and important also feel this. The operating force that maintains the unequal relationship is the force of prestige.

Yet the weak and the powerful are not two separate species; both are subject to the blind and impartial play of force, which is ultimately external to both of them. Despite the fact that some people obviously do wield more force than others, whether through physical strength or through prestige, that force in no sense properly *belongs* to these people. Force is instead completely independent of all persons and it settles where it will. Just as there is a cyclical rise and fall of nations to and from power over a period of years, so too can we see this sway of forces within a period of days in the story of the Trojan War. The Greeks, as the first day of the *Iliad* closes, are within hours of recapturing Helen. Then they forget about Helen and instead want everything—"all the riches of Troy as booty, all the palaces, the temples and the houses as ashes, all the women and all the children as slaves, all the men as corpses." (IC, 36) The Greeks think they actually possess force; they think they can accomplish everything. Within two days they are driven back to their ships as Hector and the Trojans gain the day; Hector fares no better than they, for instead of letting the Greeks escape, he too seeks total victory by burning their ships. The next day Hector is routed. And so the war goes on, with troops chasing each other back and forth across the plains of Ilium. The blindness of force, Weil tells us, gives birth to the idea that a blind destiny, rather than human choice and skill, is what controls the field of action.

But why does this dreary play and counterplay of force go continually on? It would seem that any reasonable observer would realize the dangers of excess, just as we always know that the television villain who boasts about how he will kill his victim always overplays his hand and comes out the loser.

As Weil sees it, the problem lies in the fact that "as pitilessly as force crushes, so pitilessly it maddens whoever possesses, or believes he possesses it. None can ever truly possess it." (IC, 31) Force is impartial in the way it settles on one person rather than another. The one on whom it settles, however, rarely has the objectivity to see this. Instead, he fools himself into believing that he actually possesses it in some unique way that is denied to others, which then leads him to think that he can exercise it in unlimited quantities. But, of course, his exercise of force cannot be unlimited, and so this belief is merely a destructive illusion that makes him foolhardy and all the more subject to the vicissitudes of force. Lack of objectivity in this case, however, is not simply the result of a miscalculation; it is in fact the effect of force itself.

We do not become deluded simply through the act of wielding force. In a deeper sense, what blinds us is the fear of losing that power. In wartime as well as in less extreme circumstances, that fear of loss of power is the fear of death, We fear death, and when faced with an enemy we are afraid that death is imminent; the power we have come to believe in as necessary to sustain our lives is threatened. Thus we feel it is necessary to destroy the enemy to protect ourselves. Yet, Weil adds, the only secure possession of power would be the possession of *all* power. Ironically, the more we attempt to gain all power—and that can only be done by the destruction of all enemies—the more we face death.

There is then a headlong rush for power, but at this point the soul—the inner self—begins to lose all aspiration for true good and for real life. All it sees is death, which by itself petrifies the soul; moreover, it begins increasingly to believe that the exercise of force is the only way out. But this is simply the illusion that force thrusts on both victor and victim. The victim's state is most obviously the result of force, but so is the victor's. Her life becomes only the play of forces over which she has no real control, despite all illusions to the contrary. She hopes for nothing but the securing of force and the things that force can bring her; what is sacred in human beings is then subordinated to force. "Such is the nature of force. Its power to transform man into a thing is double and cuts both ways; it petrifies differently, but equally, the souls of those who suffer it, and of those who wield it." (IC, 44) In the last analysis, the point at which Weil is driving in her essay on the *Iliad* is that human beings do not wield force; rather, they are simply its instruments. Human beings rarely know it, of course, but that is precisely the illusion that force passes off on them.

A war such as the *Iliad* portrays is admittedly an extreme situation in human life, although unfortunately not a rare one. But the relations between the inner person and force are not essentially different in other spheres of life. Because we fear death and nothingness, we seek to gain more and more power to fend off their threat. Then two things happen to us. First, because we can never truly be possessors of force, we become possessed by it, and because one force tends to increase indefinitely until checked by another, we rarely exercise any self-limitation in the struggle for power. As Weil saw in her political writings, this applies to the competition between nations, the drive to increase capital in capitalist systems, and the totalitarianism of the Marxist state. Even the most powerful people are driven and possessed by force. Weil, in an early essay, agrees with Marx that capitalists are more often directed by the process of the economic system than they are directors of it, but she also criticizes Marx for thinking that a revolution would change anything. As regards the Stalinist state, Weil could not believe that it was only a temporary solution until the final revolution; rather, the state too was one more example of force blindly increasing itself.

The race for power, however, is not confined to the level of institutions, but is also present in more mundane human relations as we seek to increase our wealth, security and prestige. The second consequence of our blind quest for prestige, then, is our coming to identify true human life with what is ultimately only an exercise of power. At this point we begin to see ourselves as essentially the sum of what we possess and wield, and our longing for anything beyond what we can gain by force starts to degenerate. It becomes an attempt to gain very limited, particular goods, and we idolize those goods as the rewards of blessedness—goods that are as easily taken away as they are given.

The picture of human life that is painted in the essay on the *Iliad* and in Weil's early political writings is deeply foreboding, even grim. Yet there is a twist. Although we become dominated and deluded by force, the fact that Homer could describe it so well indicates that not everyone is necessarily subject to the illusion of force everywhere and every way. Homer is able to describe the blind play of force with an objectivity that is missing in those who are subject to its power. One could never tell from the poem that Homer was a Greek, for he describes the effect of force on both Trojans and Greeks with equanimity. Although the subject-matter of the poem is bitter, Weil points out that Homer's voice never degenerates to cynical complaint. Through the implied comparison between the contest on the battlefield and the occasional descriptions of human love and home life, "the bitterness of the *Iliad* is spent upon the only true cause of bitterness: the subordination of the human soul to force, which is, be it said finally, to brute matter." (IC, 51) It is for these reasons, Weil says, that the poem is a "miraculous object"; it shows a love, a justice, and an inspiration that is absent in the soul completely dominated by force.

When Weil claims for Homer this escape from the illusions of force, however, she steadfastly refuses the suggestion that it came about solely by Homer's unaided intellect; rather, it was a gift, or, as she says, it came by grace. It is only by the gift of one beyond the play of forces that we can ever escape the illusions of force. Weil, however, did not always think this way; rather, in her early years she believed that it was an immanent human possibility to understand nature objectively without being dominated by force. She believed that through understanding nature we can at least see the reason why things happen as they do and thus accept their necessity. We can on this account at least make some moral use of any situation, and therefore remain the essential agent behind our destiny.

What caused Weil to abandon this Stoic notion? It was her experience of working in three Paris factories in 1934-35, when she began to see that the only possibility of escaping total domination was by the grace of God. It was in these factories that she encountered the phenomenon she came to label "affliction." She did not see much grace in the factories; what she did see at that time was the extreme degree to which human beings could be dominated, body and soul, without having in their power the ability to withstand that domination.

There were two reasons why Weil entered the factories that year. First, this was the way she liked to solve problems. Whenever she was not satisfied with a solution to a given problem, she thought the best way out of the impasse lay in coming into direct contact with the object of reflection. This is a method she used in her reflections on suffering and explains, in great part, why she often chose situations in which she was bound to suffer. Weil entered the factory because she apparently was not satisfied with her solutions to oppression and the problems of labor, and so she tried to experience the problem first-hand. Her biographer gives us a second reason for this decision as well; Weil hoped to find the camaraderie she assumed to exist among equals engaged in a common project. She did not find it, and the reason she did not find it is closely linked to her discovery of affliction.

Weil had certainly expected to come upon oppression and domination in the factories, but what she did not expect to find was the degree to which the machines completely dominated the lives of all those who worked at them. When she later saw Charlie Chaplin's film "Modern Times," the scene in which Chaplin is sucked into the machine and spun through its gears was not lost on her. The tedious and dangerous piece-work that had to be done at an appallingly fast rate did not allow anybody to think at all, and it so fatigued the workers that they had no inclination to do anything but drink or sleep when they left the factory. Workers rarely offered support for one another, in fact, and would often deliberately disrupt the work of others to improve themselves in the foreman's eyes. The rare times that Weil was given a simple smile, or received help when she was about to burn herself in front of a furnace, were all the more poignant for being so rare. Finally, the bullying attitude of the foreman made the workers feel like slaves. Weil recounts one episode in which a foreman who was not satisfied with her rate of work told her that he *might* keep her on if she did triple the amount in the next hour. All in all, she comments, two factors made for this "slavery": the necessity for speed, which excluded all forms of thought, including daydreaming, and the necessity for passive obedience to orders, even if two superiors gave contradictory orders.

Weil, who had always been a woman of strong will, remarked in a letter to a friend that the experience produced in her the last thing she expected from herself—docility. It was this same docility that prevented any healthy camaraderie among the workers, and even kept them from resisting authority in any meaningful way.

But, she adds, what she experienced in the factory was more than docility, it was also the loss of her sense of personal dignity afforded previously by her background, intelligence, and education. She uses an anecdote to describe the feeling that has been induced in her:

> Upon leaving the dentist's ... and in getting on the W-bus, a bizarre reaction. How is it that I, the slave, can get on the bus and ride it for 12 sous just like anybody else? What an extraordinary favor! If someone brutally forced me to get off, saying that these convenient means of transportation were not for me, that I could only walk, I believe that would have seemed entirely natural to me. Slavery has made me lose all sense of having rights. (CO, 92)

In her essay on the *Iliad* Weil leads us to understand the degree to which our personalities, whether we are victors or victims, are very much the result of the play of force upon us, including social forces. She also shows how those forces can be our undoing. In other works, however, she also understands our personalities as the means by which we participate in our culture. Where there is moderation, these personalities formed by social influences can be a source of benign esteem. But as in war so, too, in the factory she saw no moderation of force—the factory destroyed the person much as war does. At the end of the journal she kept during the factory year, Weil sums up her discoveries in these brief words:

> The sense of personal dignity that has been formed by society is broken. The class of those who do not count— in any situation—in anyone's eyes—and who will never count, whatever happens. . . . The capital fact is not the suffering, but the humiliation. (CO, 107)

Humiliation that has become a permanent state constitutes the key to affliction. Momentary insults can be endured, but when humiliation and loss of status is a constant and abiding condition of one's life, then affliction is usually present. It is for this reason that Weil never describes herself as one who was afflicted. If she lost her sense of personal dignity in the factory, at the same time she always knew that she had a caring family to return to and, because of her education, a life of the mind she could lead. Most important, she knew she could always leave the factory; the workers could not. Not only did they have to put up with daily insult, but also with the abiding thought that this was the whole of their life. The thought in itself is degrading. At some point, then, humiliation is not only an outer condition but becomes an inner one as well, for even in their own eyes the afflicted would never count for anything. It was for this reason that no one in such a condition could ever consent to affliction and be ennobled morally by it, for affliction is by its nature degrading and never ennobling.

One of the most remarkable features of Weil's treatment of affliction is the fact that she did not content herself simply with a "righteous indignation" at institutions, such as war and the factory system, that produce affliction so readily. Rather, she saw affliction as a phenomenon that is universally tied to the effect of extreme force on the soul. As a result, what is removed from the soul is any sense of hope or of power over its own destiny.

In the essay "The Love of God and Affliction," which is her most polished writing on the subject, Weil outlines some specific criteria of affliction. The first criterion is physical; affliction is always accompanied by pain. This pain need not be severe (although it occasionally is) but in fact may simply be the tightness in the chest we experience when grieving, or the aching back that comes from standing at a job all day. This pain is not in itself affliction but essential to it, because it rivets our attention on the suffering we are going through. Without the pain, we would ignore affliction to the best of our abilities.

Yet, while pain is a necessary condition of affliction, it is not the essential one. The essential condition, the one that really constitutes affliction, is the social factor. We have already seen that for Simone Weil our personalities are the effect of various forces, particularly social ones. Although in the final analysis we do not control these forces, but are rather controlled by them, we live comfortably in our belief that we do have control. Even if we do not, we still appear to exercise some influence on the world and are thus owed a certain amount of respect. Others must at least acknowledge our ability to influence or coerce them. In the afflicted, however, this ability to influence the course of events is completely taken away. Their social position is no longer one that commands respect, but merely invites further humiliation. In this sense the afflicted are completely passive and have no ability to control anything, above all their own destinies.

There is normally in human social intercourse a sort of push and pull between individuals. If one person oversteps her bounds or insults someone, she can expect that the other person will react and that somewhere along the line she will get as good as she has given. Similarly, if we are unkind or unjust to another person we can expect that he will retaliate, or that we will be punished by the law. In the case of the afflicted, however, there is not, and cannot be, any such retaliation. Their ability to resist force is nonexistent; every push they receive has repercussions deep in their souls. If we use rough humor on them, it is not a joke but a barb, which only makes them more conscious of their state. And this leads to some rather appalling actions as we keep pressing for a reaction—we come to believe, like schoolboys picking on the weakest boy in class, that the afflicted actually deserve what they get. They are thus despised and subject to further humiliation at the will of the strong. As Weil writes: "Men think they are despising crime when they are really despising the weakness of affliction. A being in whom the two are combined affords them the opportunity of giving free play to their contempt for affliction on the pretext they are despising crime. He is thus the object of greatest contempt." (WG, 153)

What about the attitude of the afflicted to themselves? It is basically the same attitudes as everyone else's. The afflicted are forced to believe that their treatment is just. Since their hatred of affliction finds its immediate object in themselves, the afflicted turn this hatred inwards and think themselves despicable, evil, and unclean. They can even go so far as to hate anybody who would genuinely help them, since they assume that only a contemptible being would touch them.

In short, the afflicted are destroyed souls. None of the natural means by which we keep ourselves from falling into psychic nothingness are available to these people. They have no real friends to give them respect, nor have they any possibility of self-respect. Their lot is that of a slave; they exercise no thought; they are simply ordered about, and have no genuine power of volition. They are scorned and reviled by everyone, including themselves.

When Weil describes affliction in this way and then calls it "hell on earth," it is clear that she intends affliction to be understood as the most extreme form of evil we can meet in this life. It is a form of suffering beyond all others. Once we call affliction the most extreme form of suffering, though, we can easily misunderstand it, for then we try to make it exclusively a matter of pain and physical disability. Affliction is neither: it does not have to involve extreme pain nor is it very uncommon. A contrast will help to show this.

In 1977 Basil Blackwell published a little book entitled *The Witness of Edith Barfoot*, which contains a tract by Edith Barfoot called *The Joyful Vocation to Suffering* as well as a number of tributes to her. Edith Barfoot was in many ways an extraordinary woman. In adolescence she became a victim of rheumatoid arthritis and before long was housebound and bedridden, remaining so for the rest of her life—she was eighty-seven years old when she died. She lived in constant pain and, to add to her woes, went blind at the age of seventy-three. Yet thanks to the spiritual direction and care of various members of a nearby monastic community, the Cowley Fathers, her faith deepened and in time she came to see her suffering as a joyful vocation. From those who knew her, including Sir Basil, we understand that she was a constant and true inspiration to everybody to whom she spoke.

Yet, despite Barfoot's pain, a kind of pain most of us shudder at and few can imagine, she was not "afflicted" in Weil's sense of the word. She did have family who truly cared for her, as well as the friendship of the Cowley Fathers and Sir Basil. Her place in the scheme of things had not been taken from her, although having a place in the social order was probably of little spiritual importance to her. Undoubtedly she had times, perhaps even extended periods, of grave pain, yet she was not a destroyed and humiliated soul.

If we look at the sorts of people from whose example Weil first began to develop her ideas about affliction, they present a much different picture. They were, historically, her fellow factory workers of the year 1934-35. Compared to Barfoot these people were physically healthy. They went to work each day and labored all day; it was their inner life that had been destroyed. In order to keep up the appalling rate of piece-work at their machines, these laborers had to stop thinking about anything—their future, their morals, their past, their families—except the machine in front of them and the orders of the boss behind them. And both the machine and the boss were unforgiving, capable of grinding them up physically and psychologically.

The point of the comparison between Barfoot and the factory workers is not to decide who was in more bodily pain, for undoubtedly it was Barfoot. The point is, who had been completely broken? Who had ceased to be a human being? If we think of the suffering of rheumatoid arthritis as the greater evil, it is because we can only imagine it in terms of ourselves, the same selves as we are now, undergoing extreme pain. Affliction, however, is much more difficult to imagine because in affliction we actually lose ourselves. This is why we also do not usually even notice the afflicted; what we think we see is a person who is in need of help, or who needs to pull himself up by his bootstraps. But in fact there is no person left there to help.

It is the *invisibility* of the afflicted's true inner condition that makes Weil's discussion a discovery as much as an analysis. When she discusses affliction Weil is not only concerned with pointing out in a philosophical manner the extreme degree to which force can dominate a soul, she was also concerned with the fact that we normally do not even recognize affliction for what it is—the destruction of all inner life. In so far as we do not recognize affliction at all, Weil's writings on the subject are also a condemnation of the societies, the churches and the individuals which do nothing about affliction, but pass by it unseeing.

The depth of this problem was made clear to me by Richard West, the pastor of an inner-city mission church. In his daily dealings with the poor he has found Weil's understanding of affliction to be the one source that has shown him what sorts of problems he is actually facing in his work. Unfortunately, he noted in a conversation, few peope realize that the problems of the poor include affliction—especially on the political level. On the one hand, conservative politicians have tried to take away valuable support systems for the poor and afflicted on the grounds that a lack of handouts will motivate these people to work. The reasoning behind the policy fails to realize, however, that affliction is not a matter of motivation, but of believing that the weight of the entire society is sitting on their chests; they are incapable of lifting it.

Liberals, on the other hand, have attempted to provide the support, but they have failed to realize that it is not merely the lack of money and programs that keep these people beyond the pale of normal life. In both cases the help and motivation offered is something that might work for people who can affect their own destinies; the afflicted are a different matter. The solution to their problems must take into consideration their unique troubles and has to be more than an analogy to what helps the rest of us.

Both conservative and liberal politicians have therefore failed even to perceive the true nature of affliction. It is not only in the realm of politics, however, that we have failed to open our eyes. As individuals we also fail when we pass by the afflicted daily, recognizing them only to the point of realizing that we do not want to get very close to them. Our cities and even the fringes of our most exclusive universities are filled with these people. Sometimes they pass by silently and sometimes they are obnoxious, but the attention we pay to them rarely penetrates to the core of what they are actually going through inside.

However, in attempting to understand affliction, we must also understand that its occurrence is not limited to the oppressed and the poor, although it is found more frequently there; in fact, our society is constructed in a way that virtually guarantees it for these people. Affliction can occur any time a human being is subjected to extreme force, and it can occur even among the privileged classes. One parishioner I knew was an example of this; she came from a well-off and close family, was well educated, and enjoyed most of the advantages of the privileged. Yet when I knew her she had two major problems—breast cancer and pathological depression. Neither by itself constituted affliction, but in her case (although perhaps not in somebody else's) a state of affliction evolved as her body suffered and her mind became incapable of presenting clearly to herself or to others what she was going through. She was an imprisoned soul, for there was no release for her agony and no access to comfort from others. Although she was not singled out for cruel treatment, her company, far from being sought out as Barfoot's was, became something to be endured in small doses. The fact that no one was capable of understanding what she was going through—even had this been possible—alienated her from our society even further. That hurt her more deeply and made her suspicious of those who were close to her, which made matters only worse. To those who knew her, it was a psychological problem; to her it was a state which, she confessed, made death the only attractive option. When she died people made the usual comments about death being a blessed relief, although I suspect the main relief was for those of us who survived her and for awhile did not have any longer to face what the world could do to us.

Affliction can strike wherever extreme force is turned on the soul, whether that force comes from the labor system or from diseases invading our bodies. No one is completely removed from the possibility of force; no one is immune to the threat of affliction. Yet given the same set of circumstances not everyone will become afflicted, and this gives affliction a random and arbitrary quality. This very randomness is, in fact, the final key to understanding affliction.

When Weil says that affliction is random and arbitrary, she means it in a very specific sense. For Weil, this world is composed of forces which obey, out of necessity, mathematical and hence predictable laws. So in one sense the cause of a person's affliction can always be "explained." For example, we can explain how disease is passed along, how certain environments breed criminals, and how criminals act out of a certain compulsion. All of these obey physical laws, and as such even the causes which lead to a person's affliction can be explained. But that still does not explain why these causes should produce affliction—this inner humiliation and degradation—rather than simple suffering, nor does it answer the kinds of questions that the afflicted are driven to ask. For they ask a question about purpose, and this question cannot be answered by the mathematical laws of physical necessity.

The laws of cause-and-effect that we discern in the world cannot satisfy the human need for purpose. They can only be laid out in a line that the person seeking purpose finds dreary and endless. The question "Why is this happening to me?" finds no answer in these causes. Even if by using her intellect an afflicted person could discern the inner connection of these causes, she could still find nothing in them to give her hope for good, since everything that has transpired has brought her only evil. This is what is astonishing, that the world should be able to have such power over our very being. Weil did not think it surprising that simple suffering should exist in the world, since the laws of nature are such that we are normally subject to injury by many things such as disease, accident, and even other human beings. But affliction is surprising. She writes:

> It *is* surprising that God should have given affliction the power to seize the very souls of the innocent and to possess them as sovereign master. At the very best, he who is branded by affliction will only keep half his soul. (SN, 172)

The problem of affliction then comes down to the fact that not only does the material world fail to provide any ultimate purpose and good, but that it also can blindly bring us to humiliation and degradation. We do not, however, easily see this. We do not see it for two reasons. The first is that we believe we can provide for all our needs. The second is that too often when we are in a position to see that the world does not provide for all our needs, nor for ultimate purpose, we are already in a state of affliction—totally abandoned and in darkness. Even Christ himself, as we shall see, felt this. In affliction even God seems absent, for there is no sense of his presence and hope seems pointless. This absence gives to affliction an element of horror: there is nothing left upon which we can bestow our love. Thus Weil observes:

> What is terrible is that if, in this darkness where there is nothing to love the soul ceases to love, God's absence becomes final. The soul has to go on loving in the void, or at least wanting to love, though it may be with an infinitesimal part of itself.... If the soul stops loving it falls even in this life, into something which is almost equivalent to hell. (WG, 172)

Affliction is a moral and religious problem, and that is how it will be discussed in later chapters. But at this point what we need to understand is that if there is such a thing as affliction in the way Weil describes it, then any notion that the world can provide for our needs as human beings has to be seriously called into question. And if the world cannot provide these things for us, what can be the answer to our longing for perfect good?

THE SUFFERING OF LOVE

"When Pity herself becomes afflicted, where can she turn for help? It would have needed another Christ to have pity on Christ in affliction."

"The Love of God and Affliction"

If there is a lesson to be learned from our coming to understand the existence of affliction, it is the one Weil penned in her notebooks a few years after the factory experience: "If there were no affliction we should be able to believe ourselves in Paradise. Horrid possibility." (NB, 294) The world of material cause-and-effect by itself cannot meet our aspirations for purpose and an ultimate goodness; without some rude awakening such as affliction provides, we might delude ourselves into thinking it does. That delusion is a "horrid possibility"—it means that we would never even look for purpose beyond this world.

Yet if Weil understood this when she left the factory, at the same time she did not automatically assume there is something of value beyond the material world. At the time that she left the factory, Weil was deeply perplexed. Although she recognized to a greater degree than ever that we hope for a good that the material world cannot provide by itself, she had less hope of finding a good corresponding to that hope. Indeed her recognition of our desire for an ultimate purpose and good only increased her sense of despair; her eyes became open to the fact that nothing her mind could apprehend in this world would ever correspond to that longing. Thus between our finite world and some ultimate and final good there is an immeasurable gulf, or "void," as she calls it. And so after having left the factory physically exhausted and mentally without confidence, Weil was, in her own words, "in pieces, body and soul."

The resolution to her quandary came to her in an unexpected fashion, in a series of mystical experiences. The first, we are told, took place when Weil went with her parents to Portugal and while there, on a solitary excursion, came upon a small fishing village, which she says was "also very wretched." It was the evening of the festival of the village's patron saint and there was a candlelit procession around the boats, accompanied by the singing of ancient hymns. While watching the procession, Weil realized that there was something in Christianity that was poignant and beautiful and which *belonged* to all this wretchedness—both hers and the village's. She writes: "There the conviction was suddenly borne in upon me that Christianity is preeminently the religion of slaves, that slaves cannot help belonging to it, and I among others." (WG, 67) Weil began to realize that we cannot move from earth to heaven, but that God does cross the void and comes to us as we are. It was in the recognition of God's incarnation in Christ that Weil found perfect good coming to us.

A further deepening of her sense that Christ's goodness belongs in the midst of suffering came to Weil in 1938 while she was attending the Holy Week services at the abbey of Solesmes. Throughout the week she was suffering from the migraine headaches that plagued her all her life, yet despite the pain she was able "to find a pure and perfect joy in the unimaginable beauty of the chanting and the words." (WG, 68) It was at this point, she says, that she was able to conceive, by analogy, how one could love divine love even in the midst of affliction. She also notes that it was during these services that the thought of the Passion of Christ entered into her being once and for all. Weil does not fully explain what she means by this, but it is not difficult for us to surmise that in the midst of her own despair over the problem of affliction, as well as her own pain, she found in Christ's sufferings something that corresponded to all she had come to understand about affliction during the factory years. The thought that a person who is as innocent as Christ was would undergo affliction willingly haunted her, and became a subject of constant meditation.

It was not only the thought of Christ's passion that entered Weil's being during these services; it was also a sense of his presence. During that week of services Weil met a young English Roman Catholic who introduced her to the English metaphysical poets, and because of him she memorized George Herbert's poem,

The Suffering of Love

"Love," which she constantly recited to herself. It was during one of these recitations, she says, that Christ himself took possession of her. Contact with God was not something she had expected or even thought possible; yet it was not something she could deny once she had experienced it. The love of God had passed into her for the rest of her life. It was a love, however, that she would always associate with suffering; not only with her own, but with all suffering.

What had happened at Solesmes was the unexpected. Weil did not find a way to cross the void; instead, she found God had crossed it in order to come to her. As a "solution" to her difficulties she felt it was indubitable, but it was not one that could be approached by the mind alone. Indeed, she says, "neither my senses nor my imagination had any part [in the experience]; I only felt in the midst of my suffering the presence of a love, like that which one can read in the smile on a beloved face." (WG, 69) The certainty of the reality of the experience was not an intellectual certainty, any more than we can be intellectually "certain" that somebody is kindly disposed to us because he smiles. Instead, it is a certainty that comes from the heart, through which the look of the world is suddenly changed for us.

God's unexpected coming, and the certainty of his presence at a time when suffering obsessed her and wracked her physically, gave birth to the insight that perfect love and goodness can be present even in the midst of suffering. In fact, her conclusion went further; she claimed that love and goodness are perfected in suffering and are not at all alien to it. This idea becomes particularly important in Weil's religious thinking for two reasons. First, it allows her to make a connection between perfect goodness and Christ's suffering on the cross. As she pondered affliction in the years to come she became increasingly convinced that in the light of the cross, affliction and suffering could have a deep connection to ultimate purpose, rather than defeating it.

Second, the connection she makes between suffering and goodness caused her to think of the problem affliction poses not along the lines of traditional theodicies, which try to reconcile the existence of evil with an omnipotent and good God who creates the world, but rather in terms of what the experience of affliction and suffering might offer to spirituality. As she writes, "The extreme greatness of Christianity lies in the fact that it does not seek a supernatural remedy for suffering but a supernatural use for it." (GG, 73)

Weil's idea that goodness is perfected in the suffering of Christ's cross, and that affliction can have an important use in spirituality, gives her thought its clearest significance for us today. Weil was not merely interested in furnishing theological and philosophical explanations, but was deeply concerned with the spiritual practice of living truthfully—even if it means suffering. Rather than think of affliction as an ugly mark on the otherwise beautiful face of creation, a mark which needs to be explained away, she would have us see its real use. For Weil, affliction illustrates the true nature of God's love and the real significance of the creation. In order to see the nature of that love, however, she also says that we must be willing to accept affliction as a reality of creation instead of disavowing its existence. Any theology, philosophy or spirituality that does not take affliction into account—that does not consider the depths to which God's love must reach—cannot help but miss the central truth and inspiration of Christianity. If a theology, philosophy, or spirituality does not consider those depths, it is merely superficial and offers little real help to those who are genuinely in despair.

How then does affliction disclose God's love? For Weil, affliction lets us see that God's love and perfect goodness can be present to us even when we have no power and prestige. In fact it allows us to realize that presence in a much clearer way. As long as we wield power and influence, believing that we can make our own way in the world, we tend also to put our hope for good in things that are merely within our grasp. In affliction, however, that belief is no longer open to us. Affliction forces us to realize that nothing is within our grasp. Goods, such as prestige and power, for which we had hoped in the past, have become through their very absence the instruments of our humiliation. Yet affliction, on the other hand, offers us the opportunity of standing before God with no obstacle or illusion between us and him. If we continue to love and hope then, even when nothing around us gives us reason to hope, we can love God himself and not a substitute. It is also then that his love can be received in all purity.

The opportunity that affliction provides for a pure love between us and God does not mean that we can desire affliction; that would be perverse. Neither does it mean that affliction automatically leads to a pure experience of God's love. As Weil notes, affliction is *not* a divine educational method. Instead, the only way we can possibly make use of affliction is through the example of someone like Christ, who continued to love even in the absence of God, when that person can communicate such a love to us. When that love is present we are able to be carried beyond what human nature can desire, love, or even accept if left to itself. It is then in Christ's cross that this perfect love is experienced; he is both the example and the mediator of the love of God. For Weil, Christ on the cross is not Hegel's "martyr for truth," positive thinking's "success story," or an unjustly treated revolutionary. Instead, he was truly afflicted—degraded, humiliated and thought worthless by everybody around him. Christ also felt that way about himself; he was not even the mistakenly maligned King of Glory, confident in himself. Although we refuse to recognize affliction for what it is, and thus find it hard to accept the same condition in Christ, Weil's insight is clearest when she points out how intensely Jesus must have felt the absence of God and of any good purpose when he cried out, "My God, my God, why have you forsaken me?" There certainly have been others who have suffered more pain, but no one, Weil thinks, has ever been so abandoned and devoid of hope as Jesus was on the cross. She writes: "When Pity herself becomes afflicted, where can she turn for help? It would have needed another Christ to have pity on Christ in affliction." (SN, 192) The force of the world, physical and social, was turned on him and he was humbled, abandoned, and without hope of deliverance.

Yet, although Christ was afflicted as any other person might be, there are still some essential differences. Whereas most human beings try to wield power, even benignly, in order to secure their places in the world, Christ did not. From a human perspective, the force that leaves its mark on us in affliction comes about because we have failed in the attempt to maintain our power. When we lose we tend to become bitter, because we think we have been treated unfairly and we assume that the world is a hateful place that conspires to degrade us. Like the warriors of the *Iliad*, we deceive ourselves into believing that force is not blind and that we can have special control of it. Weil tells us, on the contrary, that Christ is not deluded in his suffering, for he has never attempted to gain power nor made its exercise the way to achieve his own good. In Jesus' concern for the poor and oppressed, he is not tempted to raise these people up by destroying the rich. If Jesus spoke against the evils of wealth, St. Mark tells us that he also looked upon the rich young man with love. Jesus criticized the Pharisees, but he did not establish justice by trying to destroy them.

In this sense, Jesus had the clear sight to accept the consequences of life in this world. In choosing not to possess force, he chose not to love one thing of this world more than another, and loved everything in creation by refusing to play off one part of the created world against another. He did not use force to resist force; instead, he chose to accept, without complaint, the exercise of force upon himself. If his life generated forceful reactions in others, instead of letting them loose in the world he accepted them on himself. This did not make him simply passive. In seeking perfect good Jesus did not condemn force. He merely refused to hallow its blind possession and exercise, even if that meant accepting on his own shoulders the consequences of living in a world made of force. In so doing he neither railed against God for unfair treatment nor complained about the created world that had the power to reduce him to affliction. In obedience to his mission Jesus accepted this affliction, as he accepted the entire force of the creation that was turned upon him, as the Father's will.

Through being obedient in this way, Jesus continued to love the Father. Even though he could neither see nor understand

The Suffering of Love

anything that corresponded to the good he had set out to accomplish, he still continued to love in the void that was left and refused to deny that love. Jesus did not mistakenly identify that good with any earthly good, nor try to find any compensation for his sufferings, as we often try to do to remedy our sufferings. He simply remained as far removed from the Father as anyone could be and continued to love. Even though God was utterly absent, Jesus still loved and remained faithful, although he had no hope.

How is Jesus' action redemptive? It is redemptive because ultimately his love, even when God is absent, is in no way diminished. Undiminished, it reunites the Father and Son, even though one is in heaven and the other is in the depths of affliction. Weil tells us that our longing for a perfect good, which can only be met in God, is always fulfilled whenever we hold onto that love in every circumstance and do not cheapen it by finding substitutes for God. God will always come to those who truly love him. Weil, borrowing a phrase from the Gospel, says the proof of this is that when we ask our Father for bread, he does not give us a stone. The very same love which unites the three persons of the Trinity into one God continues to unite them, even in separation.

> The love between God and God, which in itself is God, is this bond of double power; the bond which unites two beings so closely that they are no longer distinguishable and really form a single unity, and the bond which stretches across distance and triumphs over infinite separation. (SN, 176)

When Weil talks about the cross, she is drawing on a number of sources for her insights. Undoubtedly, her discussions with Father Perrin informed her on doctrinal points; she draws on her own experience and her reading of the Gospels; and she blends all this with her own Platonism, particularly in developing an all-embracing doctrine of mediation. But what is most important for our understanding of how she can see love triumphing over separation, especially in affliction, is the mystical notion of "spiritual nakedness."

Human beings wear clothes for two reasons. One is, of course, for warmth and protection; the other, to help us project an identity to those around us. Yet, at times, that identity we project does not truly reflect our inner being. It is for this reason that Plato, in the *Gorgias*, tells a myth of how souls judged after death are required to come before their judges naked so that the judges would not be deceived by outer appearances. The metaphor of "spiritual nakedness" is an extension of this idea. When nothing stands between us and God, our true selves can be joined to him and clothed in his goodness. We, however, do not easily give up this veil, for our positions and prestige give us security in the world and a way to manage our daily bread. In affliction, though, the veil is torn away. If we continue to love in affliction and not wish for our old costumes back, because God crosses the void to all who truly desire him, then there is an opportunity for a pure, undiluted contact of the soul and God. In that contact, when there is nothing between the soul and God, spiritual unity can be achieved and our deepest longings for good fulfilled.

When Christ then refuses to clothe himself in power and prestige and actually undergoes affliction, a perfect unity is achieved between him and the Father when he continues to love. In this way, even the most horrible act of evil need not separate us from the love of God, for at the very moment that it takes place our attempted hold on the world is broken. If we continue to love when we no longer know what exactly it is that we are loving, then God comes to us and joins himself to our suffering. Then that suffering is no longer an unmitigated evil, but an opportunity for a full revelation.

> They alone will see God who prefer to recognize the
> truth and die, instead of living a long and happy existence
> in a state of illusion. One must want to go towards
> reality; then when one thinks one has found a corpse, one
> meets an angel who says "He is risen." (SN, 194)

Christ, however, is not just one who has remained steadfast in affliction and thus a single example of one who has found a way to

God through evil. He is also the mediator who brings God's love to us, for he suffers for the life of the world and not for himself. He accepts affliction so that no condition on earth, including affliction, may be removed from God's love. Because Christ has accepted affliction—not for his own use but ours—God's love can be present in our lives. That is why Weil claims it is in the cross that we can see what God's goodness really is and how he bestows life.

Weil's claim is clearest when we understand the centrality of the cross for all of her theological thinking. When theologians talk about God they often assume a sort of chronological exposition that begins by considering the nature of God, then Creation, and then the mysteries of the faith such as the Incarnation, Crucifixion and Trinity. This scheme is to some degree a convenient device for textbooks. In Weil, however, there is a clear sense in which her understanding of the nature of God and the creation depends upon the cross, for she understands God's goodness and the method of creation as a similar renunciation of power. It is through God's renunciation of power that we are given the power to exist.

In order to understand the mediation of the cross better, let us look at Weil's treatment of creation. Before God created the world, Weil tell us, he was the whole of existence. In creating a world, however, he must cease being everything. He must curtail himself and his absolute power. Weil shows how he does this when she describes the manner in which God creates—not by power of force, but by the renunciation of his power. When he willingly renounces his power out of love for a world that until creation has only existed in his mind he ceases to be all and a world can come into being.

> Because he is creator, God is not all powerful. Creation is an abdication. But he is all-powerful in this sense that his abdication is voluntary. He knows its effects, and wills them. God has emptied himself. This means that both the Creation and Incarnation are included with the Passion. (FLN, 120)

It is by his renunciation that a world comes into being. But, Weil continues, this does not mean that God withdraws from his creation and remains separate from it, letting it go any way it might. Instead, for Weil, this renunciation implies a "crucifixion" in God, for, she tells us, the world is created by this renunciation of power *and* by a simultaneous separation of the Father and the Son. Borrowing an image from Plato's *Timaeus*, she claims that in this separation the Son is incarnated and crucified on the body of the world. He becomes, in Plato's terms, the "Soul of the World"; he is the one who gives life to the formless void. Or, in the terms of the ancient Christian Fathers such as Athanasius, he is the Logos which gives the world its reason, form, and its light and life. Thus it is by the Son's willing separation from the Father and his renunciation of power that he gives the world life—his own life. When the Son then incarnates himself as a man, and undergoes the historic crucifixion, he gives up all divine prerogative and completes within the creation itself the process by which God gives life to what had not previously existed. Whatever true life there is in this world, it is the life Christ has sacrificed and given to others.

There is an analogy between the life that is given to others by the divine sacrifice and the raising of children. When we raise children our goal is to let them become adults, which is to say, to let them have their own individual lives in the world. They will not have these lives, however, if we determine directly every thought and movement they might make. If we did, they would be, at best, only extensions of ourselves. We, therefore, withdraw our control so that they may take charge of their lives. At the same time we hope that they will not become self-absorbed and that they also will learn to give something of themselves in order to let others have life, whether it be their own children, their fellow human beings, or even their parents. It is thus that we might understand God's love, if we also understand that he, unlike us, has had to give up everything.

This idea of giving life to another through renunciation goes to the very heart of the nature of divine goodness. The nature of that divine goodness is, in the first place, to be selfless. God's

The Suffering of Love

goodness is not something he keeps isolated in himself, but is continually and freely giving to others. Even in the Trinity the divine goodness is shared out. In the creation, God gives of himself by renouncing power and sacrificing the Son. Divine goodness was then perfected when on the cross Jesus gave up all to become the lowliest among us. Life was given to the world through this selfless sacrifice in which the Son is incarnated in the world. By his being a part of the creation from the very beginning he is the life of the creation.

The Son's incarnation and crucifixion should not be taken alone, however, in understanding how he gives life and goodness to the creation; that life also comes from the love that continues to exist between the Father in heaven and the afflicted Son on earth. When Christ willingly gives up his unity with the Father, he does so out of love and obedience to the Father's will that a world should exist with purpose and goodness. Yet he continues to love the Father even in his affliction and, in turn, across the infinite distance of separation of the Father's love comes to him. The two loves thus rejoin Father and Son, but now the creation is part of that love because the Son belongs to it.

Weil thus extends the idea of Christ's affliction on the cross as the place where God and the human soul are united, to affliction being the key to creation itself. Although we inevitably see creation, incarnation and crucifixion as three separate steps, for Weil the essence of the first two are contained in the crucifixion. In other words, the very creation depends upon the cross as its foundation. When Weil talks about the creation coming about because of the Son's being crucified on "time and space," she understands that God's love goes out to the world not abstractly, but concretely—he shares the suffering of the world by actually suffering its forces. But even this crucifixion on time and space would remain abstract to us if Jesus did not actually suffer those forces on the cross. It is for this reason that Weil claims the cross is ordained from the very beginning. She points to this cosmic dimension of the cross by quoting the Apocalypse: Christ is "the Lamb slain from the foundation of the world." Thus creation begins in God's ordaining of the cross, for the Son is "crucified" as the Logos in order to undergo two further crucifixions—the Incarnation, whereby he renounces his divinity, and the historic crucifixion in which he gives up his life and perfects all love.

Weil uses a metaphor taken from music to explain herself further. If we stretch a string between two posts we find that, when plucked, it will sound a note. It is called the open string. If we then press a finger down on this string, it will sound a different note—but the second note will stand in a direct mathematical relationship to the first. For instance if we press down the string at its midpoint, we find that it produces a note an octave higher than the open string and so defines two notes an octave apart as having a ratio of 2 to 1. Every other note in the scale also has a definite ratio to the open string, and correspondingly a relation to all the other notes. Weil bids us think of these notes as every single thing in creation, which are all related to each other. If then, she adds, we think of the open string as the love that binds the Father in heaven and the Son on the cross, we can conceive how all the intermediate points of life between fullness and emptiness can be harmonized in the divine love. Each point has a relation to every other point through having a relation to the divine love, and thus through Christ's mediation on the cross, God's love can be present in all of creation.

This analogy is important because it stresses that no condition is outside the divine love; every condition is part of the divine harmony. Even affliction, which seems evil and no good part of creation, has a use. In fact affliction is extremely important because it stands at one "post," and without it the string could not vibrate. But it is not merely affliction that now has a use, for so does every other part of creation—if we but open our eyes to see it. The tragedy of existence lies in our not opening our eyes, assuming instead that we and our infinite aspirations are the poles from which the string vibrates.

The problem of how we open our eyes and avoid the tragedy of limiting God's love is one that will continually occupy us in the next chapters. It is important to realize that Weil in constructing her analogies and theory of the cross is not just intellectually satisfying idle curiosity. Instead, she wants to indicate that the world is not an evil place, nor does it have to create an obstacle between us and purpose and everlasting goodness. To accuse Weil of thinking it does is to accuse her of a Manichaeanism of which she is not guilty. To be sure, the world by itself cannot provide us with ultimate purpose, but if we give up our attempts to control the world and accept it as God created it, with all its forces—even those which produce affliction—we, like Christ, accept his will.

To accept the world and to accept not only the possibility of affliction but its actual coming to pass, is the first step in opening our eyes to God's true nature as well as our own. Although we think we know what it means to be finite beings in a world of force, we really don't. Too often we think that we control that world, as if we were beyond it and as if we could provide all purpose by ourselves. But we are not beyond force. We do not understand ourselves or the world until, like Christ, we have accepted this world as it is, as what God intended.

Being able to accept the world does have tremendous meaning both for the problem of affliction and for how we are to live in the world generally. For those who are afflicted and who accept the blind forces of creation—the very forces which obey God's will—and continue to love, even when love seems impossible, affliction becomes a means of perfect love between the soul and God. Affliction is still suffering, but it ceases to be a losing contest with nature. Even when we are not afflicted, we often see the world as setting up obstacles between us and our desires. We then either wish these obstacles did not exist at all or we try to manipulate them to our own ends, as if they belonged to us. What we fail to see is that these obstacles can also be the very laws which keep us alive and give us life. It is the same world that produces us and our projects that also produces cancer cells that call a halt to those projects. If we can accept these realities, instead of competing with them, we begin to strip ourselves of illusion.

We rarely strip ourselves of our pretensions about the world, especially those we have found so effective in keeping us alive and secure. If, however, we renounce them and consent to the world as it is, then at least in our minds we have created a whole world of beauty, even though like Christ, it has meant accepting our own nothingness. If we continue in our effort to love without plotting and anticipating what must happen in order for us to find the world acceptable, then the love which binds the soul to God crosses the void and gives us the true life that we can also give to others.

THE WEIGHT OF LOVE

"There are people whose manner of seeking God is like a man making leaps into the air in the hope that if he jumps a little higher each time, he will end up staying there and rising into heaven."

"Some Reflections on the Love of God"

"My love is my weight."

Augustine

In a book published in the last century entitled *Flatland*, Edwin Abbott described through a playful fiction just how difficult it is to apprehend dimensions of our lives of which we are not usually aware. Using as his protagonist a triangle that inhabits a two-dimensional world of length and breadth called Flatland, Abbott portrays the entrance of a sphere, a solid, three-dimensional being, into that world. The poor triangle, of course, cannot see the sphere as a sphere because he cannot perceive depth. But after being taken on a tour of lands with either a single spatial dimension or none at all, and trying to explain to their inhabitants what life in Flatland is like, the triangle begins to catch on to what the sphere is talking about. For the triangle begins to find a release from its flat thinking in a world that includes depth, although it is unable actually to see that world.

In a more serious but similar way Simone Weil, upon discovering that God's goodness belongs by nature to suffering, became aware of another dimension to affliction—indeed, to all of life. The dimension she discovered is the reality of God's love in the world.

Normally we tend to see affliction as a condition that not only brings a crashing halt to human purposes, but also gives us reason to think that the world of force in which we live is completely alien to our hopes for any good whatsoever. When affliction is found to have a use, however, we can see that our hopes and the world are not necessarily at cross purposes, for we can see a side to the natural world, even in affliction, that signals another dimension to our lives. Force does not have to thwart us; it may be the very gateway to what we have longed for.

For Simone Weil, then, the fact that goodness can be found in suffering, and that affliction has a use, means that our lives are made up of something more than force. They also have a spiritual dimension. We are not simply the creation of force and our lives are not lived only in the sphere of force. There is also within our lives, and within the world as a whole, the divine love that exists always and everywhere alongside, and even within the forces of the world. The only problem is how we are to discover that love within the world. Or, to put it in Weil's terms, how we are to discover and live life according to divine grace in the natural world of "gravity."

Throughout Weil's works there is a key distinction between gravity (or the related term, "necessity") and grace. Gravity, on the one hand, signifies the unbroken chain of natural causes and forces to which all created beings are subject as material, biological, and social entities. Grace, on the other hand, indicates the divine movement of love and goodness that penetrates the world of force and makes harmony out of its various elements, and which enters the soul and binds it to God. Although Weil has a tendency (for reasons which will become apparent) to oppose the two terms when she is trying to get us to see and to respond to grace, she understands both to be continually operating in the world. In this sense, the world has two aspects—physical gravity and spiritual grace.

But if Weil wants to distinguish these two aspects she also calls on us to make a further distinction, namely, a distinction between the world as it is in itself and the way *we* see the world and act in it. Although gravity is not in the final analysis opposed to grace, we have a tendency to confuse the two by trying to make the workings of gravity satisfy our need for purpose and goodness. For example, it is inevitable that as physical beings we exercise a certain amount of force in the world, yet we easily come to believe that we can accomplish everything we need by force. Unfortunately for us, our longing for purpose and goodness cannot be satisfied by gravity, only by grace. When we confuse the two, Weil says, we become subject to "spiritual gravity" and our souls are directed by the forces of gravity instead of responding to grace. Then our lives become only one more link in the chain of natural causes, and are no longer the means by which goodness penetrates the world.

In the essay "The Love of God and Affliction," Weil makes a brief comment which illustrates this spiritual gravity. She writes: "Those whom we call criminals are only tiles blown off the roof by the wind and falling at random. Their only fault is the initial choice by which they become those tiles." (SN, 177) In other words, a pattern is established in a criminal's life that the criminal has no more control over than a tile falling off a roof has control over its fall. Gravity or natural forces control both. If we tell a lie, for example, we often find that when we are questioned on that lie we are obliged to tell another lie to cover up the first. When that happens we find ourselves trapped in a pattern that we are no longer controlling. The pattern is not predestined, for as Weil notes there is an initial choice in the matter, but once it is established forces outside ourselves determine what we will do.

Weil also gives another example of this spiritual gravity when she reflected on people's behavior during rationing in World War II: "The people who stood, motionless, from one to eight o'clock in the morning for the sake of an egg, would have found it difficult to do so in order to save a human life." (GG, 2) In such an instance, it was not the case that rationing had deprived these people of any food; it only deprived them of a variety of foods. Because they had pathetically pinned their entire hope for good on the luxury of one egg, these people found extraordinary strength to wait in line to get it. But the spiritual strength needed to save a human being was beyond them.

What Weil means by spiritual gravity is similar to St. Augustine's metaphor, "My love is my weight." Augustine, like Weil, often used spatial metaphors to indicate what is of God and what is not; what is above is nearer to God and what is below is farther away from him. When he then says "My love is my weight," Augustine means that how we love and what we love either raises us toward God or lowers us. If we love only created things, and with a "worldly" love, we do not grow in divine love. If, for example, I love a friend simply because she looks good on my arm when we go out, my love is "weighty." Or, as Weil put it, our spirituality becomes no more than another element of the material world that has become all-important to us. If, on the other hand, we love others first for what they are, and not out of self-interest, our love ceases being weighty and raises us. Neither Augustine nor Weil would say gravity is evil; indeed, it is an integral part of the created order that God finds good. What *is* evil, however, is that we allow ourselves to become so attached to the things of gravity that our lives become little more than cogs in the wheels of material cause-and-effect. When this happens the natural forces of the world take on an evil hue, not because they are evil, but because our love has "put force on the side of baseness." (GG, 2) What is natural now seems evil to us because of our sin in loving the creature in place of the creator.

The sin of this misplaced love also has inner repercussions. Weil thinks that once we have entrusted ourselves entirely to gravity, both our values and inner being can be destroyed by blind forces of nature that do not respect values simply because they are ours. Weil, drawing on folklore, gives an illustration of the sort of problem she sees in our choice to find value in the natural world alone. She recounts the stories of giants who cannot be harmed because they have hidden their souls in an egg, which is in a fish, which is in a deep lake guarded by dragons. In each of these stories, however, she notes that someone always discovers the giant's secret and breaks the egg, killing the giant. She then comments: "The giant has made the mistake of hiding his soul on this earth. A young Nazi does the same thing. For a soul to be secure, it must be hid elsewhere." (EL, 102) Physical things, no matter how permanent or secure they may appear, are always subject to the pressure of force and can never be indestructible. In order for us to find a permanent goodness, then, we must look elsewhere. We are, Weil thinks, faced with a choice of where to trust our soul—in gravity and its forces, or in grace.

The problems of trusting one's soul to gravity alone is something that we have already seen in Weil's essay on the *Iliad*. She claimed there that despite their beliefs to the contrary, it was not the warriors who really controlled the course of the battles but a blind impersonal force rooted in nature. The warriors were not aware of this, however, because they wanted to believe they were in control; otherwise they would have had a hard time continuing to fight. Their desire to fight, though, is only indicative of where they had put their trust and hope for purpose—in the sacking of Troy and the capture of its riches. As a result of this desire they are deceived, in effect losing control of their destinies, and the mechanical forces of war come to dominate them even to the point of their foolishly believing that they control the situation. To trust one's soul to gravity alone is to give one's self over to the vicissitudes of the purely natural and material world. It is also to let our wills become only one more link in the chain of natural cause-and-effect. The people standing in line for an egg are no more in charge of their lives than the warriors of the *Iliad*.

Something has gone drastically wrong in such cases, for the spiritual realm is excluded from our lives and we do not see any alternatives other than submitting to gravity. Yet why do we not see alternatives? The reason, Weil suspects, comes from an egotism that lets us believe that we are very important people and that everything of importance in the world is centered on us. When we believe this, it is also natural for us to believe that we are exempt from the necessities of cause-and-effect. This latter belief seems logical because if we believe that everything of importance is centered on us, would not the world cease to have importance if anything happened to us?

Weil gives a fascinating analysis of egotism which connects it to the problem of gravity. Egotism, she says, obeys the law of perspective. Just as when on a clear day we look up into the sky and it appears to be a bowl inverted over us, with the center directly above us wherever we go, so too, Weil says, that it always appears to us that we are the moral and metaphysical center of the world. The value of everything else seems to be determined by us, as the center. Thus things that are closest to us, such as our family, our social group and our choice of ideology are of the utmost importance; what is farther away, such as people on the other side of the globe, is correspondingly less important. At least this is how things appear to us. It is the perspective of most individuals. However, the spiritual fault, and Weil would call it sin, comes into play when we believe that we really *are* the center of value. We then come to see the world, including our own lives, solely through the perspective we embody; we ignore the fact that everything else also has a similar point of view. In that case the gravity of our nature dominates even our inner being, so that we look no further for purpose and value.

When we come to see the world that way, our egos become all-important. At that point we will do any number of things to protect and enhance ourselves, since the stability of the world appears to depend on us. But, of course, at the same time the very ego that we take such trouble to protect then prevents us from seeing any other value, and thus the good things we hope for come to be identified with what feeds and protects our egos. It is, for example, not uncommon for marriages to break apart simply because a wife will not cooperate wholeheartedly with her husband's unbridled ambition. To him, his projects and goals are all-important; nothing else counts. Non-cooperation then seems like treason to him, a good reason for dissolving the relationship. What he cannot possibly grasp are the things of importance to her, such as her own life and the lives of their children.

It becomes clear how pervasive spiritual gravity is when we look at it in the light of the ego and the "law of perspective." All of us are subject to a self-centered perspective, and most, if not all of us, consider valuable only those things which are close to us. This becomes even clearer when spiritual gravity is contrasted with the life of grace. Most of us obviously fall far short of it. Whereas the life dominated by gravity is characterized by a self-centered perspective, life lived according to grace is in *no* sense marked by a desire to expand our power, nor by a belief that we are the center of the universe. Instead, the life of grace is marked by an attempt to renounce our individual perspective as being all-important. It is an attempt to understand the importance of all other beings, whether they are close to us or not.

When gravity and grace are contrasted, it also becomes clear that when Weil speaks of the quality of gravity she does not have in mind only extreme cases, such as criminals, communist dictators, and capitalist bosses. She is also thinking of any instance where the motive for our action is founded and based in the ego, despite the occasional good things that come from these motives and actions. The scientist who finds a cure for a dread disease, but who carries out research mainly in order to receive prizes and praise, is "under gravity"; so is the preacher who inspires us by his Sunday sermon yet the whole time is patting himself on the back for his fine delivery and erudition. When we can see that such people are also examples of living under gravity, then it is not difficult to imagine how it can be present in any human situation, particularly when there is the possibility of receiving praise, prestige, or wealth. It is present in any situation that feeds our vanity. In fact, Weil would say, gravity is present in the soul whenever there is any personal attachment or personal vanity in our motives. This gravity is what keeps us from loving God. Borrowing an image from St. John of the Cross, she notes that the slenderest thread tied to a bird's leg can keep it from flying. Similarly our love of the things that feed our egos, even the most innocuous, can weigh down our love.

It is when Weil begins to make this strong contrast between life lived under grace and life lived under gravity that many of her readers hesitate. We find it hard to follow her in her strong insistence on renouncing the ego in all matters of spirituality, for that renunciation clearly does mean giving up our attachments to many things that are dear and valuable to us. It is at this point in her thinking that charges of psychological ill-health are brought against Weil. However, she has two important reasons for insisting on this renunciation: our profound power for self-deception, and the example of pure love found in Christ's death on the cross.

First, it is in those cases where some good comes out of what we do, even when we do not have pure motives, that we can allow ourselves to be most deceived about what is truly good. It is, for example, very easy for us to defend our pet political beliefs on the grounds that, if enacted, they will do the most good for the country as a whole. We feel particularly virtuous if in fact the policies we support do some good. Yet the whole time we may have simply been voting our own pocketbooks. We do not easily recognize, though, that this is what we have been doing. When we are doing some limited good for others, even though we are doing that act for our own sakes, we can easily believe that we are doing only good. But as St. Augustine pointed out, this belief is the kind of spiritual pride that is at the root of sin, for it is the belief that we can play the role of God by providing good things both for ourselves and for others. Weil understood clearly that the motive which derives originally from the ego could encourage this pride and allow us to deceive ourselves about what we are really doing.

This fear of pride and self-deception might appear as mere scrupulousness on Weil's part, however, were it not for her second reason for renunciation. This reason is one that comes from Weil's understanding of Christ's example of having loved the Father perfectly even while he was afflicted on the cross. When Weil says that Christ was afflicted in this way, there is no question but that she sees him as redeeming the worst of all possible evils in human life. But there is further significance to what Christ does. By establishing a perfect bond of love between himself and the Father in affliction, he provides the paradigm of love. The bond of love uniting the soul and God is created when the soul has consented to have nothing but the love of God for its life. Affliction in this sense, while being a real possibility, is also the prime symbol of how one is to love God, that is, with *all* one's heart, mind and strength. Maintaining our attachments to any of our own personal concerns means giving less.

The idea that affliction provides the prime symbol of spirituality does not weaken in the least bit the significance of the cross, as if it were *only* a symbol. Instead, the idea adds force to Weil's sweeping criticisms of the degree to which both the institutional church and secular society are the products of gravity rather than the fruit of grace and justice. In comparison to the complete and willing renunciation of Christ, a renunciation of his own life by which he gives life to others, both church and society (Weil contends) have fostered their own particular finite ends, and even increased and sanctioned self-deception. It is important to see how.

When Weil wrote to Father Perrin concerning her hesitations about joining the church, she expressed doubts about the legitimacy of subscribing to definite doctrinal formulations; these, she thought, would hamper her intellectual vocation. But she also added a more general criticism of the church in stating that she feared the warm feeling of belonging to a group that considers itself exclusive. This is a feeling she attributed to French Roman Catholics, although she certainly did not limit it to them. To be more exact, however, it was not the feeling itself she feared—indeed, she says, she would have liked that—what was dangerous was the way that the group deceived itself into thinking that the feeling came from God, from righteousness, rather than being the natural effect of belonging to an exclusive social group. This belief, she thought, gives the social aspect of the church over to the "Prince of this world"—it easily leads us to invoke God to hallow our personal projects and prejudices, even to the point that we think we can define all truth, and assume that he concurs in our definitions. Yet all the while that we think we have been increasing holiness, we have actually only been trying to increase our feeling of belonging. The feeling, however, is natural and not supernatural, and thus the perfect good that is held out as an ideal turns out to be only what gravity provides. Weil roundly criticizes this ersatz spirituality with the comment: "There are people whose manner of seeking God is like a man making leaps into the air in the hope that, if he jumps a little higher each time, he will end up staying up there and rising into heaven." (SN, 157)

When we believe that the "warm feeling" comes from God, it is all too easy to seek God merely by trying to increase the feeling—unless we pay heed to the example of complete renunciation. To the degree that the church has not seen Christ's love in affliction, therefore, and has instead become a haven of security for insecure egos, its goals are no different from any other institution's. However when the church has prepared people to live without the false supports of the ego, especially in the extreme case when affliction forcefully takes them away, it has prepared them for the perfect love of God.

It is not only the church, however, that presents a mistaken ideal of what is good and allows us to confuse true good with the natural workings of gravity. It is also our society and the way we learn values in it. One of Weil's chief examples of this is in our use of language. Language, she argues, is something which allows us to think, but because it already has a structure before we learn it, we cannot help but embody that structure in our thinking. That is, we cannot decide by ourselves what words will mean; we must use them as they are commonly understood, and that already commits us to a certain point of view. This is a philosophical point she shares to some degree with Wittgenstein. There is also a moral point to the observation, however. In so much of our contemporary culture language gives inordinate value to things such as wealth, prestige, and success and so we come to think of ourselves, even quite unconsciously, as valuable to the degree that we are wealthy, prestigious or successful. At the same time other value words, such as obligations to others, or obedience, are debased. Thus even through the language we learn as children we are subject to social influence as to what we shall consider good. There are, of course, also less subtle means by which our values are shaped by the society, such as direct social pressure, our economic system, and our national identity.

This social influence that Weil was ever aware of and wrote about constantly—she called it the Great Beast—should not be misconceived, however. It would be easy (we do it all the time) to blame "society" for our ills, but this is too simplistic for two reasons. First, it is not the case that society is a larger-than-life individual that decides to "deceive" its members. Society is simply a collection of its members, one more force among many, and we ought not to expect that it is anything else. Second, it is the individuals in the society who believe these false values and maintain them. It is often the case that the complaint about what "the society expects me to do" is raised only when that expectation clashes with our personal whims.

There is an example in Weil that is helpful to illustrate the way we are subject to social influence and the way we contribute to it. Throughout her writings Weil is always critical of both the ancient Romans and the Hebrews because, she says, they worshiped power, particularly the power of the social collective. The

Romans, she says (and to a certain degree she is correct), made no genuine advancements in art, literature or mathematics, having stolen whatever of these things they did have from other cultures. Where they did make advancements was in military arts and cruelty and law. Yet even this last was not a point in their favor, since their form of law consisted in the main in the "just use and abuse" of property, which is to say that their conceptions of justice, even justice to persons, dealt only with material objects.

Weil's condemnation of the Romans is harsh and unforgiving, and there is little doubt that she had no admiration for anything they did. This was not just a personal quirk. She brings the subject up constantly in her writings as a corrective to *our* worship of power. The Romans are, in this case, used as an historical example of cultural depravity. However, Weil also brings the subject up constantly because of our cultural practice of holding the Romans up for the admiration of school children and as the standard of glory for most political endeavors. "La gloire de la France" echoes "The glory that was Rome's," but few other countries are any different. Hitler's idea of the "Thousand Year Reich" was patterned on the Roman example. The slogan was effective because people already had been conditioned through schooling to admire reigns like this. When we admire such a cruel civilization, we not only contribute to the idolization of power but also continue it personally and individually by deliberately making our civilization an outgrowth of Rome. The point is that power seeks its own means of continuance, but we do not merely acquiesce. Instead, we are subject to it to the degree that we each contribute to it.

There is thus a plain and obvious contrast between life lived under gravity and life lived under grace. In contrasting the two, however, Weil is not making an attempt to separate the sheep from the goats. Rather, in describing spiritual gravity and contrasting it with grace, she is describing our everyday failure to recognize the divine love that is as much a part of the world as the presence of gravity. In describing the life of grace, she is trying to describe a life that recognizes and loves the divine love. But a more important question still remains. How do we transform a life that is entirely enmeshed in the world of gravity into one of the world of grace, especially when our expectations of love and even our ideas of God have been formed under the influence of gravity? How do we avoid the temptation of trying to jump higher to reach heaven?

The change occurs by means of grace itself, which first comes to us while we are influenced by gravity and then transforms us into the image of Christ. Weil uses a metaphor to describe the process. If, she says, just once and even in a small way, we leave our egos unprotected, as we do when we appreciate something of beauty for itself, God comes and plants a small seed in our souls. If we do not choke the growth of that seed by refusing it, it will grow until "a day comes when the soul belongs to God, when it not only consents to love but when truly and effectively it loves.... The love within it is divine, uncreated, for it is the love of God for God which is passing through it." (SN, 181)

Even the apparent efforts we might make towards helping the growth of the seed are the result of grace, Weil uses another analogy here, one that likens grace to the sun. Solar energy is the only power that can overcome gravity. By synthesizing it, plants grow; in turn, animals use it and grow by eating plants. Finally, when fossilized animal remains are converted into gasoline, it powers our airplanes. This is not an energy we can create. We can only receive it. But Weil says we can dispose of ourselves in such a way that we do receive it. The farmer, for example, plows his fields so that they will receive the optimum amount of sunlight. Ultimately, however, even the energy the farmer uses to work his fields comes from the sun through the plants and animals he has eaten. "In the same way, the only effort we can make towards the good is so to dispose our soul that it can receive grace, and it is grace which supplies the energy needed for this effort." (SN, 151)

It is at this point that Weil introduces the key notion in her thinking that gives content to the process of the growth of grace—the idea of paying attention. It is the act of paying attention which first opens us to grace, and it is the increase of attention that finally brings us to God's full presence. The importance of attention for Weil is captured when we recall her saying that attention is the only faculty of the soul that gives access to God.

Attention in the first place for Weil means simply what it says; it is the turning of one's mind to some object or thought. But there is something extraordinary in that act, for if it involves genuine attention the mind is totally turned to its object and does not consider itself at all. A momentary suspension of the ego takes place. The object of thought is not considered as something that might be useful to us, nor is it considered in the light of how it might fit into *our* lives. It is purely and simply considered for itself. The act of attention is an unself-conscious realization of the object itself.

Attention of this sort is not a rare occurrence, and most of us at some point or other in our lives have experienced it. We may not have realized what has happened, though. I remember a discussion I once had with my father in which he told me about how as a boy in a rural Minnesota town he once came across the man whom everybody thought of as the village idiot. Because the man was obviously confused and frightened, since he thought he was lost, my father put his arm around him and led him home. Ironically, later in the same conversation my father lamented the fact that he may never have performed an altruistic act. True attention is like that. It focuses so entirely on another that we forget to think of ourselves and count our own good works.

It is the act of paying attention that creates the first chink in our egos and allows the seed of grace to be planted in us. In cases like this either beauty or goodness, or our neighbor's need, may cause us to suspend our egos momentarily and really look at what is in front of us. This suspension of the ego is not, however, something that we ourselves do; it is the reality of something outside of us. Here Weil says that beauty, whether in individual beings or actions or, more important, the beauty of the world as a whole, is extremely important for spirituality. Beauty, she claims, is a snare for the soul, set by God so that he may enter it.

It is not the case, of course, that we can pass automatically from a momentary act of attention to beatitude. Instead we must develop the quality and intensity of our ability to pay attention until it becomes the substance of our life. There are many ways to do this. In the essay "Reflections on the Right Use of School Studies with a View to the Love of God," which she wrote for the girls at a Roman Catholic school, Weil shows one of these ways.

In this essay she tells us that the proper end of school studies is the development of the attention, and that whenever there is a genuine effort of attention, it is never wasted. If, for example, we bring our attention to bear on the solution of a mathematical problem, even if we do not find the solution, the effort is not wasted. Through such efforts students learn at least to reject all the ways they would like to see it solved. Honest ignorance is an advance; it clears our minds of false opinions and prepares them for seeing what is really in front of them. The student has suspended her ego and let the object penetrate her mind. This penetration is the essence of attention, for "attention consists of suspending our thought, leaving it detached, empty, and ready to be penetrated by the object . . . above all our thought should be empty, waiting, not seeking anything, but ready to receive in its naked truth the object that is to penetrate it." (WG, 111, 112)

The faculty of attention that needs to be developed in school studies, Weil says, should not be confused with the muscular efforts of contracting the brow and looking very serious. Neither should it be undertaken with a view towards grades, prizes, and promotions, nor because the subject matter piques the student's interest. All of these attitudes defeat true attention; they revolve around the self, and not the object of study. School studies, then, if they are to help develop attention, must be conducted solely on the basis of a desire for the truth of the object. What that truth may be we have no way of knowing ahead of time, nor should we project any of our own personal hopes on it regarding what form it will take. The desire of attention has to be a desire stripped of all our intention, except for our desire that whatever is revealed to us be revealed in truth.

School studies develop one type of attention that we can readily recognize. But, Weil goes on to add, they develop only a preliminary, "lower" sort of attention. The true spiritual attention towards which studies must ultimately be directed is the kind found in prayer. Prayer is here for Weil "the orientation of all the attention of which the soul is capable toward God." Briefly put, attention is prayer. In the desire manifest in prayer lies the sole power of putting the soul in contact with God; ". . . desire directed toward God is the only power capable of raising the soul. Or rather, it is God alone who comes down and possesses the soul, but desire alone draws God down. He only comes to those who ask him to come; and he cannot refuse to come to those who implore him long, often, and ardently." (WG, 105, 110)

The equation of attention with prayer is a feature well recognized in most treatments of Weil's thought. Unfortunately, in many cases its significance is misplaced. Most writers do not sufficiently recognize that this equation of attention and prayer is the means by which Weil breathes new life into traditional spirituality without trying to replace the tradition itself. Too often attention is emphasized at the expense of prayer, and churches stress the need to pay attention to our neighbors and to the world as a matter of prime importance. The idea that we should pay attention to neighbors and to the world certainly exists in Weil, but she is equally serious in her belief that all attention finally needs to be brought to bear in prayer, in attention to the transcendent good that lies beyond us. In paying attention, our naked desire for purpose and good is directed to the absolute good alone. Without the attention of actual prayer, the idea of attention can take on the spiritual falseness so glibly expressed in sentiments like "My whole life is a prayer." One's whole life is not a prayer unless undivided attention is paid to the good above and beyond the world.

The entire Weilian quest for genuine spirituality as I have been trying to present it is an attempt to put the human soul into contact with the absolute good that is both the basis of its life and the goal of its desire. This quest cannot be reduced to moral and spiritual self-improvement. As the English novelist Iris Murdoch puts it, we cannot seriously change the commandment "Be ye therefore perfect as your Father in heaven is perfect" to "Be ye therefore slightly improved." The whole point of Weil's spirituality is pure contact between God and the soul without any obstacle between the two, especially the obstacles our egos so easily put up. The failure to see prayer as the essential means of that contact, and the necessary preparation for it, is rather like a pianist practicing difficult pieces for a concert and then failing to show up.

If contact between the soul and God is the basis of Weil's spirituality, we can better understand her identification of attention with prayer. Prayer, for Weil, is not petition, at least as we normally understand it; it is not directed to divinely helpful provision for our day-to-day lives. Prayer rather is the concentrated attention that desire brings to the sole object that will satisfy it. In short, attention and prayer consist in the love of God. It is the union of God's love for us and our love for God, a love which ultimately has originated in God himself. If there is petition in prayer, it is that we accept the Father's will and love, and desire it wholeheartedly.

In her meditation on the Lord's Prayer found in *Waiting for God*, Weil tells us what sort of petition is appropriate prayer. The petitions in the Lord's Prayer, she says, run parallel to the changes that take place in ourselves when we pray. At first, we pray that God's name be hallowed. We thus begin with acceptance of his holiness. We then express a desire by asking for the coming of his kingdom, but quickly return to acceptance in asking that his will be done, not our will. In these opening petitions of the Lord's Prayer we fix our attention solely on God, whereas in the last three we fix our attention on ourselves—"to impel ourselves to make these petitions real and not an imaginary act." (WG, 226) In these last three we pray for our daily bread (Weil translates "daily" as "supernatural") and forgiveness of our debts. That forgiveness, she says, comes when we forgive the debts of others, or, in other words, when we give up personal claims on the world. Weil translates the Greek literally as "debts" because she believes that often in our relations with others we conduct those relations as if we were *owed* something. When we forgive these debts, we give up our self-centered claims on the world. It is also then that we stop directing our own narrow way in the world. Our direction is now determined by God alone and thus we conclude the prayer that we not be led into temptation. We end with this petition because we have now consented to be led wholly by God's grace, not by our own wills. This last petition, then, is one that is offered as we are transformed; it expresses a desire for protection, but desire now comes from humility and from the acceptance of God's will in all things. Weil concludes that the Our Father

> is to prayer what Christ is to humanity. It is impossible to say it once through, without a change, infinitesimal perhaps, but real, taking place in the soul. (WG, 227)

Weil herself prayed the Lord's Prayer daily with the fullest possible attention, and the presence of Christ became a daily reality for her.

It is through paying attention, particularly the attention that is paid in prayer, that the quality of our love changes. We cease being the victims of gravity and begin to be led by God through his grace. The transformation does not take place overnight; it is gradual but, Weil adds, it is certain. Gradually there is a renunciation of the limited perspective our egos provide, a letting go of all attachments except for our desire and love for God. At that point, it is pure love and nothing but love that passes between God and the soul. The stage at which renunciation of the ego is completed, and the terminus of this *via negativa* reached, is what Weil calls "decreation." The term is apt; it describes a point at which we cease trying to be only what we possess by force and prestige. It is also a point at which we cease trying to control our own lives by dominating others. When we have consented to be nothing and to possess nothing in the world we can be everything God's love will make us, for we belong to him.

The stage of decreation is one where we are waiting for fulfillment by God alone. The stage of decreation is thus to be distinguished from attention, not as something distinct from it, but as the state in which attention has become the sum and substance of our being. Attention (*l'attention*) can be episodic, even when we sustain it for prolonged periods. Waiting (*attente*), however, is a state of *permanent* attention in which at every moment of our lives our own personal desires are suspended and we desire only and always the reality of things as they are, and not as we want them to be. It is at this point we wait patiently for the object to reveal itself. And ultimately we wait for the absolute good for which we hope. In time, Weil says, if we wait patiently God will come.

The best example of this relationship between decreation and waiting, besides that of Christ's passion, is found in Weil's interpretation of Aeschylus' play *Electra*. *Electra* is the second part of Aeschylus' trilogy, the *Oresteia*. In the first part, King Agamemnon returns from the Trojan War only to be murdered by his wife and her lover. His son Orestes, the rightful heir to the throne, flees; his daughter Electra remains in the royal house now ruled by her treacherous mother and her mother's lover. Electra's life is a miserable one, and her misery is deepened by her belief that Orestes, the one person who can set things right, is dead. Yet despite what amounts to a certainty on her part that Orestes is dead, she refuses to renounce her love and desire for him. In the scene that constitutes nearly the whole play, she bewails her fate while holding what she believes is the urn containing Orestes' ashes. Finally Orestes himself appears. Electra does not recognize him and he does not at first reveal himself. Instead an exchange takes place between the two that we find painfully long, because we cannot understand how Orestes can be such an unfeeling cad as to let Electra continue in the misery and pain of believing her sole hope is dead.

Weil gives this exchange a mystical interpretation, for she tells us it contains an allegory of our waiting and of God's descent to our souls. "Electra is obliged to stretch her detachment to its extreme limit, even to do violence to her love for Orestes, before Orestes reveals himself to her. She must let go the urn." The urn, which she believes to be her last connection to Orestes, has to be released in order to stretch her detachment to the limit. It is when she lets go the urn and still continues to love, and even increases her love, that Orestes reveals his identity to her. "This is the sort of fidelity raised to the point of madness which compels Orestes to reveal himself. He can no longer restrain himself from it; he is overpowered by compassion." (IC, 17)

Waiting is something we can do without much difficulty when we expect the person for whom we are waiting to come at any moment. The waiting Weil is talking about, however, is more than that; it is a waiting where we cannot reasonably expect the other person at all. If we still continue to wait, though, hoping without hope, Weil thinks we will have made pure fidelity and a naked desire for that person the essence of our lives. There is no one else and nothing else we want then. But, she adds, that desire is not really pure until, like Electra handing over the urn, we are willing to give up every concrete hope. Often when we expect and wait for someone we wait not only for her, but also for what she brings. We therefore do not really wait for that person wholly, but also for the benefits that accompany her. When we give up our expectations, however, and still wait, it is the person alone we desire. To do this is to seek the kingdom first.

Weil's development of the Electra story is a mystical interpretation of her ideas on attention and waiting. Yet it also has a very deliberate bearing on the use that can be made of affliction. Affliction can destroy, but it can also have the effect of decreating us and bringing us to waiting. If we are prepared to hand over all of our life, affliction only completes the process.

First we must be prepared for this, however; otherwise, affliction is a tragic waste. In a sense we must already have developed a sublime indifference to our ego's welfare in favor of the good for which we ultimately hope. Without it we can only experience suffering as a bitter personal loss. That indifference to our own welfare, moreover, is by no means an indifference to the world around us. As we shall see, our preparation consists precisely in caring selflessly for all of creation.

THE SACRIFICE OF LOVE

"Pure friendship is an image of the original and perfect friendship that belongs to the Trinity, and is the very essence of God."

"Forms of the Implicit Love of God"

"If anyone wants to be a follower of mine, let him renounce himself and take up his cross every day and follow me. For anyone who wants to save his life will lose it, but anyone who loses his life for my sake, that man will save it." Although this saying of Jesus, one of the few repeated in all four gospels, is a paradox, it clearly expresses an idea that is at the root of Christian spirituality. For Christians it is not the person who thinks only of self who will find true life, but the one who gives sacrificially. If we renounce ourselves for the sake of others, we will find the ultimate good that we so desperately need. The idea is clear—yet how *do* we take up our cross every day?

Simone Weil makes it clear in her writings on spirituality that we are faced with a choice. Will we live our lives blindly, controlled by the mechanical necessities of force and prestige, or will we live in accordance with God's grace? She also makes it clear that there has to be a change, a renunciation of self, which will accompany the choice of grace. Renunciation is found at its fullest in waiting, she claims, and it is there that the human and divine are bound together in love. Yet "renunciation" is perhaps the wrong way to put it; when it comes from love and for love, renunciation is more properly termed "sacrifice" because this sort of renunciation is always for the sake of something or somebody else. For Weil, whether she is talking about God's own sacrifice in creating the world or our sacrifice of an ego-based perspective, the love involved in sacrifice is always to give life to something outside ourselves.

Weil, of course, did not invent the notion of sacrifice. It is a central idea in the New Testament and in discussing Weil we must always be aware that she describes sacrifice by means of her deep appreciation of the cross. But if Weil is correct in stressing the importance of sacrifice in Christianity, then she is a rare voice offering both a philosophical theology and a devastating criticism of contemporary theology and spirituality. If churches and the theologians are offering succor to the ego by teaching us how to be self-affirming, but are not at the same time teaching us how to give up that ego voluntarily, then we are not only resting in self-deception but also running another risk. It means we will not know how to make use of conditions such as affliction, when, against our will, our egos are devastated.

Weil's criticism is valid if we assume that she is right in putting sacrifice in such a central place. But numerous essays on Weil have argued either that she is wrong to do this or that she has only uncovered half a truth. The objections to what Weil is doing can be divided into two sorts, one theological and one psychological.

Theologically, one need not go so far as to deny that Weil has uncovered one truth of Christianity in the notion of sacrifice, nor deny that this is an important notion to be recovered. But is this *the* central truth of Christianity? It is interesting to notice the lack of stress on many other important parts of the Gospel in Weil's writings, such as the Resurrection, the need for forgiveness, and in early works, the need for community. Without these other elements to soften and balance the difficulties inherent in sacrifice, it would appear that we arrive at a religion of perfectionism that is impossibly difficult for the weak human wills it is meant to save, even if their growth is by means of grace. If this is the case, then the practical effect of religious practice is towards a kind of Manichaean dualism that sees the human spirit and the world, if not completely at cross purposes, at least as two alien things.

Rarely, however, are the criticisms of Weil's thinking on sacrifice confined to strictly theological categories. Since Weil herself attempted to live a life of sacrifice, criticisms are often brought to bear on her psychological state. One such critic has suggested the ambivalence of sacrifice in Weil, noticing the consistency of Weil's ideas on sacrifice with what may be pathological features of her personality. Weil's desire for perfection is linked to a morbid sense of failure; her inability to recognize

The Sacrifice of Love

common friendships as valuable is linked to jealousy of her brother in competing for their mother's affection; sacrifice is linked to an unhealthy wish for death and a denial of her own womanhood. Weil, a woman, describes her salvation in terms of obedience and slavery, and even consciously employs metaphors of sexual violence. All this, it could be argued, results from an overemphasis on sacrifice that can be balanced only by the resurrection and by an "*alliance* between matter and emotion . . . which have put the elements of Christianity, that she explored all too thoroughly, in their place."[3]

I think that it is entirely possible that Weil, *in her own life*, may have had a tendency to concentrate on perverse versions of sacrifice. Unless we claim that she achieved perfection, and I do not, then it is no surprise to find gravity mixed with grace in her life, as it is with most of us. I also think that she was aware of this, as for example when she writes to Father Perrin and says that she commits the sin of envy whenever she thinks of the cross. In the essay "The Love of God and Affliction," Weil writes that it is perverse to desire affliction. In this case the assessment of her friend Gustav Thibon may well be correct: "Her humility is still partly inspired by a *negative* preoccupation with self: she carves her ego by hollowing it out as the proud carve theirs in relief. The ideal would be to make it a perfectly smooth surface on which one could glide without stopping. . . ."[4]

Yet even if Weil falls prey in her life to the morbid side of sacrifice, what she *says* about sacrifice can still not be discredited. If masochism is the ego's wish for death and thus a perverse attempt at immortality, nevertheless there is still a sense in which sacrifice is the spirit's wish for the death of the self so that true life may begin. Furthermore it is not impossible that both wishes can be present in one person. In the case of somebody like Simone Weil, who wanted to see without deception but who because of her physical and psychological constitution must have constantly been tempted to self-deception, the struggle to distinguish morbidity from true spirituality is one of the most significant aspects of her life. It may indeed be because she had to struggle with morbid desires for sacrifice that she learned the other side, the valuable side, of sacrifice. It should not surprise us therefore that such a spiritual writer might be unbalanced, for it is perhaps only those who have constantly to try to achieve balance who can tell us how difficult that task is.

Self-sacrifice was always a possibility for Simone Weil, but she did not simply embrace it without thought. Instead, she tried to sort out its implications. Her writings are the fruit of this sorting out; however, it should not surprise us that there was a long struggle to do the same thing in her life. Because she died so young we can only speculate whether or not she would have been able to accomplish this in her life had she lived longer.

An example of the difficulties that Weil's notions of sacrifice raise comes from her notebooks, in the text that has been called by her critics the "horrible prayer." It is a prayer for the perfect love of God, but is expressed in striking and uncompromising images:

> Father, in the name of Christ grant me this, That I may be unable to will any bodily movement, or even any attempt at movement, like a total paralytic. That I may be incapable of receiving any sensation, like someone who is completely blind, deaf and deprived of all the senses. That I may be unable to make the slightest connection between two thoughts, even the simplest, like the total idiots who not only cannot read or count but have never learned to speak. That I may be insensible to every kind of grief and joy, and incapable of any love for any being or thing, and not even for myself like old people in the last stage of decrepitude. Father, in the name of Christ grant me all this in reality.

> May this body move or be still, with perfect suppleness or rigidity in continuous conformity to thy will, may my faculties of hearing, sight, taste, smell and touch register the perfectly accurate impress of thy creation. May this mind, in fullest lucidity, connect all ideas in perfect conformity with thy truth. May this sensibility

experience, in their greatest possible intensity and in all
their purity, all the nuances of grief and joy. May this
love be an absolutely devouring flame of love of God,
for God. May all this be stripped away from me,
devoured by God, transformed into Christ's substance,
and given for food to afflicted men whose body and
soul lack every kind of nourishment. And let me be a
paralytic—blind, deaf, witless and utterly decrepit.
Father, effect this transformation, in the name of
Christ; and although I ask it with imperfect faith, grant
this request as if it were made with perfect truth.

Father, since thou art the Good and I am mediocrity,
rend this body and soul away from me to make them
into things for your use and let nothing remain of me,
forever, except this rending itself, or else nothingness.
(FLN, 243-44)

This prayer presents its readers with a problem. They can either decide it is "horrible," a perverse wish for death by its author, or they can read it as a pure wish for true life. If read the second way, we find this prayer has striking affinities with Julian of Norwich's prayer for her "bodily sickness," which has been given a highly positive evaluation by the Christian tradition. Like Weil, Julian was ever aware of the possibilities for deception in spirituality. She prayed for a bodily illness, she tells us, in order "to be purified; so as afterwards to live more according to the worship of God because of that sickness."[5] It was not the sickness itself she desired, but truth in her love of God.

It is also important to remember that after Julian's sickness, these sorts of petitions cease. Weil, who at the time of her "horrible prayer" was virtually the same age, did not of course live as long as Julian of Norwich. We can read Weil's prayer as the expression of an aberrant personality or as the thought of perfect love and obedience, in which the "I" (in French the ego is *la moi*, the "me") disappears and the petitioner is transformed into Christ's substance. Yet we do not even have to go as far as that to make a hard and fast distinction between what is unbalanced and what is pure spirituality. One person can embody both. The only question is, which dominates?

There is a way, I think, by which we can distinguish. One kind of mysticism that has been justly criticized by numerous writers takes the form of a flight from the world, characterized by denial and nihilism. Even if another world is the "true" one in this kind of mysticism, that world has nothing in common with the one in which we are created and in which we live. Flight to that other world undercuts the reality of this world by making it only a matter of stepping stones. Under the guise of true life, this sort of mysticism does make death and nothingness the lords of the universe.

Yet this is not the sort of sacrifice Weil is talking about. Sacrificial love for her is not a way to escape to another world; it is a way to bring another world into this one. Throughout her writings the goal of spirituality is to incarnate God's love in our lives here and now. God's love for the world is not perfected except through the Incarnation and the cross. Similiarly our love should not be an attempt to mount the skies, but to embrace the reality of the cross. But at present our difficulty is that we do not see either the cross or affliction as real possibilities, denying that we are limited creatures of matter subject to matter. Thus we are split between what we think we are and what we actually are. As Weil writes in commenting on the *Symposium* of Plato, "Our vocation is unity. Our affliction is to be in a state of duality...." (IC, 110) Perhaps it is only Christ on the cross who can unite love and matter; he alone does not resent his being flesh, nor does he cease to love God when reduced to the state of affliction.

There are two metaphors of spiritual progress that Weil thought best expressed the true nature of spirituality, and they are helpful in showing her thinking. These metaphors are the analogy of the cave in Plato's *Republic* and the dark nights of the soul of St. John of the Cross. With both images the mystical ascent begins in a condition of darkness that is far from truth and clarity. Plato, for example, likens our condition to that of

The Sacrifice of Love

people chained to a wall in a cave and forced to watch shadows cast on a blank wall in front of them, rather like a movie theater. He tells us that these inhabitants of the cave assume that the shadows are tangible and real; they even have contests among themselves to judge what the shadows are. These cave-dwellers are quite happy with their lives, while thoroughly deluded about the true nature of the world. Suppose, then, that one of them were to be freed and dragged out of the cave into the sunlight—an image that Weil thinks suggests grace. Because his eyes are not accustomed to the light, and everything he sees would look unfamiliar, the cave-dweller would at first assume that he knew less than before and would think that he had been led into a world of fantastic fictions.

Similarly, St. John of the Cross likens each step of spiritual progress to a journey on a dark night: each step involves giving up the old comfortable and familiar landmarks by which one had previously been guided on the way. Both Plato and St. John speak of the end of the journey, however, as one where the soul can gaze directly at the full light of goodness. It then knows how to distinguish between truth and illusion. Weil, in commenting on these passages, however, notes one more significant step in this journey that is often missed by other commentators. Once the good has been contemplated, it is necessary that we return to the world of darkness in order to lead others out of it. In fact, Weil adds, it is in the very nature of the good to return to the darkness, just as it is a mark of the spiritual person to help others. In this way she makes it clear that there is no ultimate escape from this world and no way of denying this world's significance.

By the way she understands these images of Plato and St. John, Weil clearly indicates that what dominates in her ideas on sacrifice is not nihilism. In each writer she understands the ascent to begin in sacrificing numerous things, such as living harmoniously with the opinion of our neighbors, that we have used to make our lives comfortable. The sacrifice, however, does not reject this world; rather, it is made so that the substance of our lives may become God's own love. We are then ultimately to use that love for the sake of others in this world.

Love accompanies every act of sacrifice in a twofold way. First, in the struggles of the soul between gravity and grace each act of sacrifice and attention—for paying attention is a sacrifice—increases the presence of grace. The life of self-centered perspective becomes less of a permanent possibility with each new act of attention; waiting for God becomes a greater possibility. Second, each act of sacrifice, if it is genuine, brings goodness into the world around us, for it is a giving of ourselves. When we sacrifice ourselves, it is not merely to trade for a greater reward; paradoxically, as Christian thinkers have continually observed, each act of sacrifice is only good for us when that act is done for others. Attention bears fruit for us in nakedness and waiting when it is truly attention paid to another person, rather than to the *idea* of ourselves paying attention.

Certainly individual acts of sacrifice and attention do not put us face to face with God. Until sacrifice and attention are the substance of our lives, they alternate with gravity and as a result we struggle. This is why somebody like Weil, who would not have claimed perfection for herself, can seem to exhibit such inconsistency in her behavior. However, acts of sacrifice and attention may build on each other until they become the substance of our lives. It is for this reason that Weil found it so important to describe sacrifice and attention in her essay, "The Implicit Forms of the Love of God." Although throughout many of her writings Weil was concerned to show the ideal, it is here in this essay more than anywhere else that she shows how the ideal of love is not only reached, but how it penetrates our progress.

In the course of his intense discussions with Weil during the year 1941-42, Father Perrin became aware that the two of them shared a deep commitment to serving those who were "seeking a way to the light of Christ." Because of this shared concern, together with his belief that Weil—although not baptized—had a greater sense of the universal mediation of Christ than most Christians, he pushed her to express this sense more clearly. Learning that she was shortly to leave France, he continued to press her on the issue and on the eve of her departure Weil responded by giving him a number of essays, including "The

Implicit Forms of the Love of God." In this essay, Father Perrin tells us, she set out to show how the commandment to love God, stated so categorically in the gospels, can be obeyed even when we have no direct experience of God. In short, it is a description of how the love of God can be present to all people.

For Weil, the ideal of love consists in the love of God flowing to us and returning to him in a direct and unhindered way that is possible only in spiritual nakedness. This is a state she calls "explicit" love, for the soul stands before God directly without pretence or any other mediating factor save God himself. That is the ideal, however, and we do not attain it easily. Rather we must grow to the stature of this love by loving, and we can only love things we can understand, such as our love for our friends and neighbors. Weil calls these loves "implicit" because even when we do them in God's name, we do not fully know to whom that name belongs. Yet they really do express our love for God because they lead to full and explicit communion with him.

According to Weil, there are four forms of the implicit love of God: the love of neighbor, a love for our brothers and sisters, which is disinterested in the sense that we love these people even when they are not personally close to us; the love of the world's beauty; the love of religious practices; and the love of friends, a love for those who are close to us. Each of these is a love "in which God is really though secretly present." (WG, 137) God is secretly present because we cannot know, in the fullest sense, his presence; he is really present because the nature of these loves can only become sacrificial (rather than self-centered) through his grace. Each of these loves, even the happiest of them, shows the marks of sacrifice. It is those marks, too, which express the divine nature of these loves, and which allows them to bestow a goodness both to us and to the world that could only come from God.

The first of the implicit loves, the love of neighbor, Weil approaches in an extraordinary way: she roots it in our care for the afflicted and in justice. Citing the gospels, especially the Sermon on the Mount, and the Egyptian *Book of the Dead*, she notes that in the ancient world there was no difference between being just to other people and treating them charitably.

Moderns, however, distinguish between justice and charity, and "our notion of justice dispenses him who possesses from the obligation of giving. If he gives all the same, he thinks he has a right to be pleased with himself. He thinks he has done a good work." (WG, 139)

The key to the identification of justice and love lies in the equality between giver and recipient that justice presupposes. This equality is symbolized in the image of justice as a pair of balanced scales. The giver gives as to an equal, and the recipient responds with gratitude, not with servitude.

In practice, however, it is all too apparent that the equality needed for the exercise of justice is often lacking. To a great extent the law is an attempt to balance this inequality, insofar as it ignores differences irrelevant to the case, such as race, social position, and sex. All people are "equal before the law." The extent to which this equality obtains in a society is a measure of the justness of its laws. Yet there are cases before the law, and certainly cases in our relations with our neighbors, in which equality simply does not obtain.

The major example of inequality comes in the case of affliction. Even if we treat an afflicted person according to principles of legal justice, there is a profound sense in which there is no equality. The afflicted are no longer persons; we are. Here, despite the facade of legal principles, the strong act and the afflicted react without any volition of their own. Because their souls have been devastated, no amount of legal maneuvering is going to make them persons again; they are merely passive recipients of the decisions of others. As long as we exercise our wills upon these people, they have no alternative but to respond passively. According to natural justice, furthermore, there is no reason to seek an alternative, nor is there any culpability attaching to the one who does not recognize equality where none exists.

In an example drawn from Thucydides' *History of the Peloponnesian War*, Weil illustrates this. The Athenians are about to destroy the tiny state of Melos if the Melians do not ally themselves with Athens. The Melians refuse, invoking justice and the gods on behalf of their cause so that their town

The Sacrifice of Love

will not be destroyed. Weil quotes Thucydides' version of the Athenian reply: "Always by a necessity of nature, each one commands wherever he has power. We did not establish this law, we are not the first to apply it; we found it already established, we abide by it as something likely to endure forever; and that is why we apply it. We know quite well that you also, like all the others, once you reached the same degree of power would act in the same way." (WG, 141)

Weil does not commend the Athenians for destroying Melos, but she does say, however, that their lucidity of mind is just below that of charity. The Athenians understand that there is no equality between their power and that of the Melians, and that it would be artificial and condescending for them to invoke justice in such a case. Whatever they decide is what the Melians will have to do. The Melians, on the other hand, while understandably trying any means they can to save themselves, only paint the situation in irrelevant terms. Only the Athenians are objective. They understand that they are no different than the Melians, since they, the Athenians, could also be destroyed by a greater force. Their objectivity is not love, but clearsightedness about the sort of situation love is needed to redeem.

If the world is a balanced equilibrium, as Weil says it is, then there is a certain natural justice in the play of forces. Every excess is worn smooth over time, and the great are brought low while the humble are exalted. But if that is so, then as individuals we are left with a cold and frightening place within the world; we can be destroyed before the pendulum has swung in our favor. Yet what are the possibilities? They are found in the justice that consists of supernatural love, for this is a justice which *creates* equality even where there was none before. In fact, it creates value and it creates persons where before there were none.

The major example of the justice of supernatural love which makes people equals can be found in the way the afflicted can be redeemed. Between those who are afflicted and those who are not, there is neither natural equality nor the possibility of any. In this sense it is a delusion to believe that simply by treating the afflicted as our equals, justice will be done. When we make even a benign use of the forces at our disposal to help the afflicted, those forces do not uplift or change them. What happens to these people is what we choose to have happen, for they cannot resist us. Thus even help, if it involves our use of power, is condescending and reminds them of their condition. The afflicted, Weil claims, can only be helped if we renounce our power and become one of them, making them equal to ourselves. If by paying attention to these people we give up our privileges, and see them as human beings, then our attention becomes creative.

Weil points out a parallel between God's creating of the world and the way we can give life back to the afflicted:

> God *thought* that which did not exist, and by this thought brought it into being . . . Only God, present in us, can really think the human quality into the victims of affliction, can really look at them with a look differing from that we give to things, can listen to their voice as we listen to spoken words. Then they become aware that they have a voice. . . . (WG, 149-50)

Yet this act of paying attention is not just mental, although that is difficult enough. To pay attention to the afflicted means sharing their condition; if equality cannot be achieved by power, it must be achieved by our willingness to honor the afflicted by sharing their condition. A pastor of an inner city parish once gave an excellent illustration of this when he compared two parish workers. One, he noted, was full of good will, but came to the parish at nine and left at five and had no effect on the people with whom she worked. The other, with the same amount of good will, however, lived among the parishioners and did have an effect. God created the world by the Son's crucifixion in which he shared the world's condition; sharing another's condition is the only way we can lift him up. Thus attention, as long as it is not just a rearrangement of our mental furniture, can be creative. It can make something out of nothing.

This creative act of attention is divine for our neighbor, for it follows the pattern of bringing something out of nothing established in the beginning of the world and the cross. God renounced the divine right to command and a world began. Christ renounced his divinity and gave life to the afflicted. If we make a similar sacrifice for others, we can bring life to them. From this, true life is gained both for us and for our neighbors as we participate in the love that binds the separated Father and Son.

As an implicit form of the love of God, the love of neighbor is essentially, Weil says, a way of sacrifice and suffering. It involves accepting as our own the suffering and affliction of the world in all its pain, distress, and destroyed aspirations. If genuine, it does not seek redemption for the self, but only the redemption of others; in fact, to accept the affliction of others means to accept their hopelessness.

The second form of the implicit love of God, however, is not a way of sorrow at all. Appreciating the beauty of the natural world is a means of joy and of growth. Yet it also involves a sacrifice. When we love the beauty of the world, although it is a source of joy, we still cannot avoid sacrificing the perspective (so dear to our egos) that tells us we are the center of the universe. We, of course, do not rule over the universe in the same way that we might rule over someone who is afflicted, and so we do not renounce any real power in this love. But as Weil points out, we tend to act and think most of the time as if the universe ought to provide especially for us. We find beautiful what aids us, and ugly what opposes us. We also tend to limit the value of the world to something on a human scale, something that we can take in. Yet, Weil says, God's creation is beautiful as a *whole*, including those parts we cannot see and those parts that do not answer to our needs and wants. To give up our narrow perspective and see the world as God created it, and as he finds it beautiful, is terribly difficult. It is a sacrifice. Although we cannot *create* the beauty of the world by renouncing our limited perspective, our effort to pay attention to the world's beauty can allow that beauty to be born in our souls, a place where we had not let it exist before.

Our love of the beauty of the world is essentially a contemplative love by which we seek to appreciate and love God's handiwork. This love does, however, produce two important human activities, namely, art and science. Both of these, Weil thought, ought to reflect the sacrifice involved in this love by reproducing in themselves the beauty that we contemplate. Weil tells us that neither art nor science, when they are truly good, reproduce the artist's or scientist's perspective; rather, the artist and scientist produce in microcosm the real beauty of the universe and present it to others for contemplation.

It is not difficult for us to see the contemplative aspect in art. Whereas paintings by artists like Rembrandt and Vermeer we always find good, we can be put off by works that represent nothing more than the idiosyncratic taste of the period in which they were produced. The latter say little to us, speaking of little beyond themselves. However we can be attentive to a painting like Vermeer's "Woman in Blue," a portrait of a pregnant woman reading a letter, for hours. We find in its small subject a mystery that transcends us and tells us more about the world than many volumes of theology.

Good artists or scientists (or theologians), therefore, are those who imitate God. They consent to the independent existence of things outside themselves and, in doing so, seek their intrinsic beauty and goodness. Through a painting or a scientific experiment, then, painters or scientists make incarnate whatever they have contemplated, making of it a microcosm of God's handiwork. It is when artists and scientists do this, Weil says, that the world as a whole becomes as familiar and necessary to them as their own bodies. They react sensitively to its pressures and live in it and use it with the same concern we show for our own bodies. The world is no longer alien.

The love of religious practices is a third form of the implicit love of God. Although we may confess and avow God's existence, and love him openly, until we are joined to him inseparably and fully there is a sense in which he is not a concrete part of our lives. There may be a similarity here between Weil's implicit-explicit distinction and the distinction that St. Thomas Aquinas draws between faith and sight. For Thomas, faith is needed because we do not and cannot have in this life immediate certainty of God himself; we can only know him by his effects.

The Sacrifice of Love

Therefore we need to *believe* what he has revealed about himself. This belief, however, is not blind acceptance, regardless of the facts; it has a certainty of its own which bears fruit in our thoughts and actions. Similarly, for Weil, our religious practices involve only an implicit love of God because we still hang on to the limited notions of God that are given in church and in our culture and which our finite minds can grasp. Like Aquinas, though, Weil saw this faith bearing fruit in what we think and how we act.

Religious practices, especially corporate worship, are for Weil essentially conventions. Nevertheless they are conventions with a unique quality, for God has willingly joined his presence to our participation in them. Weil does not argue for this presence on the basis of an authoritative revelation so much as she draws on her own experience. Using the example of the prayers of institutional religion, she says that when we call on the name of God that name contains God's secret presence. It is a finite representation of an infinite reality, but through it God's love can come to us—if we speak the name with attention. Undoubtedly it was Weil's own experience of reciting the Lord's Prayer every day with absolute attention that furnished her with the proof of prayer's efficacy. Yet this way of praying is well known throughout the world's religions. It occurs in the chanting of Buddhist mantras, as Weil herself points out, but it is also well understood in Orthodox Christianity. The example of people who have become holy through constant recitation of the Jesus Prayer is held up to the faithful as something that is accessible to all.

The effect of participating in religious ceremony with rapt attention is also unique in the way that it purifies the soul. Thinking particularly of the Eucharist, Weil says that because God is present in the ritual it possesses a purity that our sin cannot defile. Weil notes that in the celebration of the Eucharist it does not matter whether the priest is sincere or even moral; the presence of Christ remains whole and unaltered. That presence does not stand isolated and untouchable, harshly condemning all who approach it. Rather, because it cannot be defiled it welcomes our attention. Unlike the forces of creation, which react in kind to our pushing and pulling, the presence of God in the sacraments does not reflect our evil back on us. Weil thinks, therefore, that when we direct ourselves to this presence and give ourselves to it with full attention, the evil in us is purified, absorbed by God just as the evil done to Jesus on the cross is accepted by him in obedience to God's will.

How does the love of religious practices involve renunciation and sacrifice? It requires us to pay attention, and it has the *effect* of sacrifice and renunciation because it does change us, purifying us of evil so that what we do afterwards is less evil. And as we are purified we begin to redeem the evil that is done to us, just as Christ redeems the evil of his crucifixion by suffering it as the Father's will without condemning his persecutors. When we are touched, then, by the purity inherent in the sacrament, then "the part of evil in the soul is burned by the fire of this contact and becomes only suffering, and the suffering is impregnated with love. In the same way when all the evil diffused throughout the Roman Empire was concentrated on Christ it became only suffering to him." (WG, 191)

All three of these loves have a universal character. They can be present in anybody, in any place, and can take us beyond our particular, personal concerns. It is for this reason that Weil calls them "impersonal." The love we express through them does not center around our personalities or egos; in fact, it leads us away from ego and personality. It is important here to understand the value of this idea of "impersonality" for Weil. For her, impersonality is not the mark of the abstract and the less-than-human; it is, instead, the mark of a goodness and purpose that cannot be reduced to our merely finite concerns. Because we are finite we do tend to reduce transcendent things such as God's goodness to terms we can fully comprehend, even though he transcends them; we also tend to reduce them to dimensions we can manipulate. Weil understood both these tendencies and, in fact, was very much aware of them because of the "personalist movement" taking place in France at the time. She saw in many parts of the movement an attempt to focus on "personality" as the center of ultimate human worth. She says critically: "The full expression

The Sacrifice of Love

of personality depends upon its being inflated by social prestige; it is a social privilege." (SE, 21)

It was in reaction to personalism that Weil insisted on the "impersonal" nature of the love of God. By stressing the impersonal nature of God she sought to establish an understanding that God is *more* than personality, not less. She also sought to make us see beyond personality and the values that comfort and support it. Whenever beliefs and practices are introduced in spirituality that succor the personality, she thought, we find it all too easy to ignore the sacrifice of self that is needed to love God and our neighbors truly.

It is for this reason, I believe, that Weil had practically no development of the doctrine of the resurrection in her writings. Clearly she believed in Jesus' resurrection but consciously avoided introducing the doctrine into her thinking. She thought that as soon as we focus on the resurrection, we begin to introduce into our thinking a way of protecting our personalities for eternity. That would allow us to remain attached to the gravity of our souls, and permit us to avoid the full and final detachment necessary to loving God wholly. It is only the one who has made the full sacrifice of personality who can fully understand the resurrection. Until we become such people we need to concentrate less on our comfort and more on the Good Friday which must take place before the resurrection.

There is something admirable here about Weil's willingness to take a point to its conclusion without balking. Indeed, her willingness to do so allows her to criticize, without being shallow, all the ways that we have developed our theology so as to avoid the genuinely difficult requirements of loving God with all our heart, mind, and strength. We dislike the idea of impersonality because it does seem inhuman, but we tend to define "human" in terms of what is more or less *comfortable* for us. But, nevertheless, we still wonder if Weil is not pushing the point too far. Are there simple joys in life which can be counted among the implicit loves of God and yet are not at the same time impersonal?

It is to Weil's great credit that she does admit such joys, although there is one period in her life and writing when she seems to resist the idea. Such "personal" joys are developed in the fourth implicit love of God, namely, the love found in friendship.

It is interesting that in the beginning of her essay, "The Implicit Forms of the Love of God," Weil is almost hesitant in adding friendship to the list on the grounds that it is not an impersonal love. Friendship is completely personal; it occurs precisely because another person does mean something to us. This is not true of the love of neighbor; when we are told to love our neighbors we should not take into account our personal feelings toward them. Friends, however, are people we have a preference for. Under this heading, although Weil herself is not this explicit, comes all of our personal loves—including husbands, wives and even children. Perhaps Weil had a hard time including this love, at first. What she says about it shows her great power of discernment even in an area of experience where she did not live as fully as she might have in her own life.

Friendship, Weil says, can come from two sources: from the good we seek in another person, or from our need for that person. Often the two motives coincide. It is when need dominates in a friendship, however, that it is prone to sour and ceases to provide us any spiritual good. For at that point we are no longer bound to the other person by love but by necessity, since she provides something we need. In such cases we rarely care much for the other person as a person, although we may still feel warmly towards her; we care about what she provides for us. If we cease needing what she can provide, then we cease caring. We can even resent our friends if it becomes clear to us that we are dependent on them, although we rarely break off such relationships.

Weil herself does not use the example of marriage to show how a relation of need can go wrong, but it is perhaps the best one to illustrate the point. Within Western society there is an ideal of love and marriage that encourages us to believe that in romantic love we find our true happiness. Often accompanying this belief is another, whereby we believe that to each man and woman there is a perfectly matched mate whom we need only find in order to be truly happy. The problem here is twofold. In the first place, because no human being is infinite, no one can provide infinite happiness for another. Infinite happiness can be given by God alone, which is why the marriage covenant lasts only as long as both shall live, and not forever. But if I expect that the person I love can and ought to make me infinitely happy, especially if I think that there is only one such person, I am bound to her simply for what she can give me. Of course, she cannot give me everything and so I am disappointed. I may even start searching all over again for the "one" person who is supposed to be able to do all this for me.

In the second place, I can cease respecting the person I love for who she is and become attached to her for what she can provide. Instead of seeking to draw out and develop the good in her that I found so attractive in the first place, I will seek to possess it for myself. I look for my own fulfillment, and only incidentally the fulfillment of my loved ones, so I never learn the hard work of respect that is necessary to maintain a relationship. What is true here of our husbands and wives, furthermore, can also be true of our friends and children.

The idea of pure friendship, as Weil develops it, is another matter. Although we are attracted for personal reasons to the beauty and goodness of other people, in pure friendship we do not seek to possess this goodness and beauty for ourselves. Rather, we enjoy and delight in it but only as the possession of someone else; we have no wish other than that our friends may enjoy that goodness and do with it what they will. This, Weil says is a supernatural friendship, for it transcends the limits of gravity. Rather than seeking to possess and control, this friendship consists in a deep-seated desire that the other person have this good. If I want the other person to change, it is only for her to be better for herself.

Paradoxically, this makes friendship a kind of separation and even a type of sacrifice. We are separate because we want our friends to be persons in their own right, not people who are bound to us. It is sacrifice because it is the renunciation of possessing the good of the others for ourselves, and this renunciation is for the sake of the other person. But, Weil adds, in the final analysis, this consent to remain separate is what binds friends together. Just as the separate persons of the Trinity are one God through love, this respect for the distance that separates friends has the effect of drawing them together.

> "Where there are two or three gathered together in my name there I am in the midst of them." Pure friendship is an image of the original and perfect friendship that belongs to the Trinity and is the very essence of God. It is impossible for two human beings to be one while scrupulously respecting the distance that separates them, unless God is present in each of them. The point at which parallels meet is infinity. (WG, 203)

Each of the four implicit loves is a form of sanctification in spirituality, but not one of them involves a turning away from the world God has created. Taken together they do not show signs of morbidity, because although all involve sacrifice, loves such as the love of the beauty of the world and friendship are also a means of joy, and joy of the purest kind.

It is when the four forms come to exist all together in the soul, Weil tells us, that they give way to an explicit love of God. This love is not simply a matter of generalized religious experience; it means that God has come in person "to possess the soul and to transport its center near to his very heart." (WG, 209) It is a state in which no other love that we might experience can hinder the flow of God's love to the world and the world's returning of that love, and where we can fully consent to this role. It is a state of perfect and willed obedience to the will of God. "We, insofar as it is granted to us to imitate Christ, have this extraordinary privilege of being, to a certain degree, mediators between God and his own creation." (IC, 195)

When we achieve that condition of explicit love, the implicit loves still do not cease as loves and there is no turning away from the world. In fact, the explicit love of God towards which Weil thinks all sacrifice ought to aim is the fullest possible turning towards the world. None of the implicit loves—of friend, of

The Sacrifice of Love

neighbor, of beauty, of religious practices—will cease; indeed, Weil says that in the explicit love of God they are all more intense than before. But one thing does change. These loves cease being merely isolated ways to reach God and become instead God's own way to the world. They become a single "ray merged in the light of God." (WG, 209) They now show forth a unity amongst themselves without losing any of their individual characteristics, the clear unity of all sacrificial loves.

We can see this unity when we look at the way joy and sorrow are ultimately linked in God's love. When we contemplate the world's beauty we must give our consent, in inward affirmation, to the world as it really is. That consent, because the world contains affliction, is consent to the possibility of our own affliction as well as that of others close to us. Yet when we deliberately share in the sorrow of others and take their affliction upon ourselves, Weil tells us that we gain a blessed contact with God. The beauty of the world is revealed to us then as it was to Job at the end of his sufferings.

It is because of her vision of this ultimate unity of love that Weil turns out to be, in the final analysis, an optimistic thinker. She can see that there is hope for transformation. This optimism comes out not only in her explicitly spiritual writings, done in the last years of her life, but also in how she thought this spirituality could be acted out in public life. In fact, she firmly believed that true spirituality must finally be worked out in public life. In this conviction Weil resembles Plato and St. John of the Cross, who thought that spirituality required a return to the cave after contemplating God's goodness. As a result, she turned the last efforts of her life toward a description of the transformation of public life, and it is in this area that her spirituality completes itself.

THE LOVE OF GOD IN DAILY LIFE

"Christianity will never impregnate society until each social category has its own specific, unique and inimitable link with Christ."

"Christianity and Rural Life"

The spirituality of Simone Weil in many important ways recalls the traditional spirituality of Christianity. Her notion of spiritual gravity recalls St. Augustine's idea that our love is our weight, and her distinction between the implicit and explicit love of God recalls St. Thomas's distinction between faith and sight. Weil also recovers the importance of spiritual nakedness and of progression in spirituality found in St. John of the Cross and other Christian mystics. In reviving this spirituality she also uses moral and psychological terms that speak to contemporary people. Rather than describing spiritual gravity in terms of concupiscence, as Augustine did, Weil describes it in relationship to our egos and in a way which acknowledges that we are creatures of our biological and social environment. Her interpretation of the life of faith takes seriously our existential concerns for authenticity, and she describes faith in terms of our action in the world. Finally, Weil's interpretation of spirituality is unique in the degree to which it takes seriously the problem of affliction; in fact, it begins there. With Christ's love in affliction as the model of the perfect love of God, she shows us the full extent of the sacrifice we should be willing to make, using spiritual nakedness to illumine the problem of affliction itself.

It would be a mistake, however, to view Weil as merely a translator of the Christian tradition. One of the most important features of Weil's thinking is her concern with the problems of daily life in the contemporary world, a concern that is apparent above all in her life-long activism. Not only did she enter the Renault factory to discover the true condition of the worker, throughout her life she also sought to find out how the poor and the marginal live their lives. After 1940 when Weil was forced by the invading Nazi troops to flee from Paris to Marseilles, she spent

much of her time there either working in the fields of the grape
harvest or with the Vietnamese refugees in Marseilles. In New
York in 1942, remote from the war, she constantly visited the
black churches of Harlem because she felt more at home
there than with the white Americans whom she found to be
so comfortable. And finally when the safety of New York was
more than she could bear, Weil managed to find passage to
London in order to work with the Free French. Her voluminous
writings on social and political matters, especially on the problems
of labor and colonization, testify to this concern with the problems of daily life.

Yet throughout many of Weil's writings this intense concern
with daily life seems to run parallel to her spiritual concerns.
Of course the two overlap. The illustrations in her religious
writings are often drawn from the realm of labor and politics, as
we can see when she describes affliction in terms of the suffering
of the workers. Also, the high sense of justice that permeates her
political and social writings is easily seen as being very much in
debt to her spirituality. But what is the exact connection, and
where in her writings does Weil treat the concerns of daily life
and spirituality together?

It is in Weil's last writings, particularly in the book *The Need
for Roots*, that she brings spiritual concerns most concretely to
bear upon daily life. Although we might wish that Weil had lived
longer and written more to express herself with greater clarity,
this work is remarkably mature in what it sets out to do. Never
at any point in her life did Weil think that the needs of daily life
and the concerns of spirituality could be divorced, and this conviction derived from her idea that even small things in life can have
significance for the soul. She could never be satisfied with an idea
that had no practical application—ideas, to be true, must be
capable of being lived out. It would only be natural, then, that
she would attempt to work out some scheme to put her theories
into practice, and fortunately she got the chance.

Weil's chance came while she was working for the Free French
in London. She had gone there in 1942 in the hope that she could
convince DeGaulle and other French leaders to accept her plan to

The Love of God in Daily Life 103

parachute front-line nurses into occupied France. This plan, if enacted, she thought would be a source of moral inspiration to the Allied soldiers as well as an act of humanity to the wounded. She knew the personal dangers, but was willing to accept them. Apparently her superiors thought little of her plan and even less of her sanity for suggesting it, so instead they set her to the task of working out problems that would have to be faced when a legitimate government was restored to France. Most likely they did not see this as a pressing need, but characteristically Weil threw herself into it until she finally collapsed, weakened by the tuberculosis that a friend has confided she had already contracted in New York. The product of that labor was *The Need for Roots*, which is hardly a typical interagency report. Instead, she offers the vision of what a truly good France could be.

There is something remarkable about this book when seen in relation to the rest of Weil's writings. Whereas she had spilled a lot of ink previously decrying the dangerous ersatz spirituality that group feeling engenders among people, especially in the church and the state, in this book Weil treats both patriotism and institutional religion favorably. This shows a deepening and maturing of her ideas for, as one commentator has noted, the strong individualism of earlier writings now makes room for a deep appreciation of the social aspect of human nature. The personal reasons why Weil wrote in this way can only be a matter of speculation. It would not be unreasonable, though, to think that her own forced separation from her homeland and its traditions, together with her sense of solidarity with those left behind, made her reflect deeply on the meaning of "rootedness" and its significance for our conversion to God and his love.

Weil's writing of this book is more than a personal reaction to her forced separation from France, however, and the ideas expressed in it are not making up for past deficiencies. Those ideas are also the fruit of a theory that Weil held implicitly for many years and which becomes explicit in her writings from at least 1939 on. That is the theory of the "intermediaries"—or *metaxu*, the Greek term she uses in her notebooks. The theory is meant to show the inter-relatedness of all created beings and their ultimate relation to God.

For Weil an intermediary is a "go-between" between God and the world; more helpfully, it is a bridge by which love passes from God to us and from us back to God. It is something by which God is indirectly present in the world. It is not always clear what sort of thing Weil has in mind when she says this, since she finds these bridges not only in beautiful physical objects worthy of our attention but also in societies, our neighbors, and even our own inner states. The best way to describe such a bridge is to return to our previous discussion of the implicit forms of the love of God and find an example there.

When developing this notion, Weil may have been thinking most explicitly of our love of the beauty of the world and the way it functions in mediating God's love to us. When we pay attention to the beauty that the entire world presents to us, we allow it to reveal the deep purpose that binds the whole of creation together. We discover a unity in existence, whereby our friendships and all of our human relationships are part of the natural world around us, as well as part of our sufferings and our joys. All are part of an ultimate purpose. Weil thinks that when we discover this, then we are enticed into loving the world as a whole and feeling a kinship with it; she uses the example of St. Francis as one who had developed this love to a high degree. Through its beauty the world itself is a mediator of God's grace, awakening in us a love that in time will bring us to his full presence.

This is not to say that we are merely passive recipients of this love; instead, it sends us out to be willing and active participants in the world. Take, for example, a scientist. A scientist who through close observation or contemplation of the world has developed a genuine sense of its beauty and purpose will not keep his insight locked up in his study. Nor will he merely manipulate his discoveries for gain—for further honors and prizes. Instead, he will attempt through teaching and writing to share this sense with others, to promote human community by helping others to have an abiding sense of kinship with the creation, a sense of belonging to it. In turn, his insights will lead to an enhanced communication of love between human beings and God.

The Love of God in Daily Life

Similarly, in the other implicit forms of the love of God, the object of our love and the love itself can be bridges between God and the world. Such loves are stages in spirituality that are already highly developed, and Weil thinks that bridges to God exist at all points in life. While love of the world's beauty mediates grace, so too does the love for very particular things of beauty, such as individual works of art or scientific discoveries that do not involve an entire cosmology. In fact, Weil contends that unless we first see beauty in small things we will probably not succeed in developing a broader and more universal love, and adds that it is often some particular beauty or friendship that first draws us out of our self-centered perspective and allows the seeds of grace to be planted. It is those seeds that ultimately bloom into a full and direct love for God.

Thus Weil sees a potential link to God in virtually everything that exists. If we recall the analogy of the musical string by which Weil sought to establish that every being in creation has a relation to the love which passes between the Father and the Son, and exists because of that relation, we can see that she explicitly argues for such a notion. However she urges two cautions when she does this. First, simply because something *can* serve as a link to God does not mean that we actually use it that way. We can and do use beauty for selfish reasons, merely to enhance our private sense of being aesthetically sophisticated rather than as an opening to a greater appreciation of its creator. Because these bridges do have potential for misuse, therefore, we must be aware of Weil's admonition that we love with a sacrificial love. We must love with attention, which is to say we are to love people and beautiful things for themselves and not for what they can do for us. Paradoxically, this is the only way that they will enhance our lives spiritually.

The second caution that Weil urges is that we are not to think that because every part of God's creation is a link to him that every link is equal. For Weil there is a hierarchy of value in the world. We do not often appreciate the idea of hierarchy: we think that whatever is on the lower end of the hierarchy is bound to be devalued in favor of what is on the higher end—as happens in many political and religious hierarchies. This, however, is not the sort of hierarchy that Weil envisions; rather, the hierarchy she sees in the world is more the relation of parts to a whole. The parts are each valuable in themselves for her, but they also contribute to a larger whole in which their real significance is made apparent. The whole, on the other hand, is dependent on the parts that make it up; it could not exist without them. This relation can be put in terms of a musical example. In listening to a symphony we may find a single musical phrase beautiful; that phrase is part of a movement and the movement is part of the symphony as a whole. The phrase, if it is beautiful, does not lose its beauty as we learn to appreciate the symphony as a whole; instead, its real beauty becomes even more apparent. The phrase by itself, without its arrangement within the symphony, however, might in time come to seem trivial. Weil argues that we must learn to see the creation as being linked together in a similar way. If we do we may be better able to understand how each thing God has created can be a bridge to a more loving relationship to the world and to him.

Weil's theory of the "intermediaries" might best be described as a sacramental view of life in which each bit of creation provides a connection to God, whether directly or indirectly. If by an act of attention we allow ourselves to see this connection and to act on it, then, as with a sacrament, we participate in God's own presence in the world and thus have communion with him. This is true, Weil thought, not only in the way we appreciate beauty and the way we deal directly with our neighbors, it is also true in the way we conduct our social life. It was with such a sacramental view in mind that Weil wrote *The Need for Roots*, in which she seeks to show how we can draw spiritual life from our social environment. In fact, she would insist, we must *learn* to draw it from our social environment. Spirituality, she believed, is always a matter of the individual's own relation to God, yet it always takes place in and is dependent upon a larger social context.

The Love of God in Daily Life

To a certain extent Weil always understood the social element of spirituality, although she saw it as a negative factor. Too often the social context in which spirituality inevitably takes place ceases to be a context, becoming instead for many people the chief source of spiritual nourishment. In this sense the particular practices and groupings of Episcopalians, Catholics, or Presbyterians become more important than the love of God at which all profess to aim. This "idolatry of the group" was one of her main reasons for refusing to join the church. Yet in the end she finally saw social collectivities as something from which sustenance could be drawn, once she was able to sort out a hierarchy of means and ends and find a less exalted value in social relations. I think also that her forced separation from France and her increasing maturity allowed her to see the true importance of social relationships as bridges to God.

Even in *The Need for Roots*, however, Weil does not pass from harsh criticism to unmitigated praise; the relationships of social life still present a major problem for her. She understands there that we must be able to make use of our societies as an intermediary link to God, but at the same time she is aware that contemporary society does not always provide the link it should. Whenever it demands total devotion or promotes individual liberties without promoting a corresponding sense of the good of the whole, modern societies tend to suck life from the people who live in them. Instead of increasing their ability to find life and love, the society will often obscure what these mean. To be a source of life society must be transformed, and that will not happen until we see our need to diagnose what specifically has gone wrong in contemporary society. The problem, Weil thought, was one that she called "uprootedness."

The metaphor of uprootedness is apt. Just as plants that are uprooted cannot take in nourishment from the ground in which they originally sprouted, people who are uprooted cannot take nourishment from the society, culture, or religion into which they were first born. Although these groupings should be a means of drawing life from the world, when people or whole societies lack roots then that life can no longer be provided. There is an important difference, however, between plants and people in this respect. Plants die quickly when uprooted, whereas people can continue existing indefinitely in this condition. In fact they may so lose touch with true value that they do not even recognize their condition or that of their society. Uprootedness does not have to mean poverty, although certain forms of poverty keep people from drawing life from their society and culture; it does mean that people who are uprooted cannot find any connection between what they are and do, and some ultimate purpose. Under these circumstances social and religious groupings can become their own reason for existing, and so point to nothing beyond themselves. The truly unfortunate aspect of this uprootedness is that the longer we live in this condition, the less we understand of purposes or goals beyond the immediate, short-sighted ones of the society around us.

Weil, I think, would say we are at a point now where we are now thoroughly uprooted, and that uprootedness is the spiritual epidemic of our age. In certain parts of the world this can be seen in the millions of homeless refugees. However it is also a problem in America. Not only has social life become increasingly secularized, money and prestige have become prime values. Uprootedness is a problem wherever the sense of belonging to the society does not lead to a sense of belonging to anything beyond it. Weil, even in 1942, was convinced that America was a thoroughly uprooted country; she claimed that the United States and Russia were chiefly responsible for the spread of the disease. Both countries, because of their exceptional historical and economic circumstances, have prospered and expanded greatly. Unfortunately, Weil continues, they have also seduced the rest of the world into thinking this expansion is normal. Thus the rest of the world, in seeking to get what these two countries possess, have lost their own traditions.

We do not have to look far for signs of uprootedness around us. Teachers can see it when students in geography classes cannot place their home state anywhere close to its actual position on a U.S. map; when in religion classes they think Judaism is a form of

Methodism (I have had such students); when their families have lived in the same area for generations, yet they neither know nor care where their family name comes from. None of this is a matter of academic ignorance—it is a matter of having no idea who they are, where they are, or where they might belong in the world or in their own culture. Often such students do not even mind not knowing these things as long as they believe that they will have secure and well-paying jobs that will allow them the material advantages of life. But, we ask, for what?

It is not enough, however, simply to see that people do not draw deep values from their culture. It is also necessary to understand how uprootedness occurs so that we might find a way to grow new roots. Weil gives a number of reasons for uprootedness. The first is obvious—it is war. Refugees driven from their homes, who have seen their traditions smashed, are plainly people who are uprooted. They have nothing left which would help them to find a place in the world. The second cause of uprootedness is also fairly obvious, for it is the oppression and alienation that takes place when one person or group greedily exploits another, or when economic forces are used as a means to establish power. In both cases, the structures of an uprooted society, far from providing mutual protection and enhancement of life, allow people to be used as little more than raw material in an enterprise that actually benefits few people, if any. Although some of the most blatant examples can be drawn from nineteenth-century factories, where workers were considered as little more than replaceable tools, others from our own time can be cited. Most efforts to break up the powers of unions, for instance, or to locate factories in non-union areas, are not designed to benefit the worker but the corporation. Workers know this and they think of themselves as unimportant cogs in the corporation's machinery. Whenever a person feels his role is unimportant in an enterprise, that he is being used, he will clearly feel alienated from it.

The third cause of uprootedness, though, is more subtle, involving as it does a transmutation of values. It occurs when money, whether as a means of subsistence or as a means of exercising power, becomes the chief motivating factor in our life.

It occurs when any action is seen in the light of the financial metaphor of the "bottom line." A striking example comes from an interview in *Newsweek* with an aspiring young businesswoman. In college she had wanted to become a social worker, but remarked that she soon realized, "If I wanted to change things I had to make a commitment to being poor."[6] She now makes a six-figure income.

Such uprootedness can also occur through ideologies that distract our attention from the present and projects it outside the conditions under which we actually live. On this score Weil tars both capitalism and communism with the same brush, for neither ideology address a worker's condition *as a worker*. Both promise the worker something else—middle-class life in the case of capitalism and a fulfilled revolution in the case of Marxism. Both promise compensatory goods, but neither finds positive value in the labor that is actually done every day. So people who work do not learn to see what value lies in whatever they do; instead, they must dream of something that is forever in the future. In an essay entitled "The First Condition of Non-Servile Labor," Weil writes that a revolution is triggered by the same sort of ambition for a better social position that capitalism promises, but here it is "transported into the collective. It is the stupid ambition of elevating all workers beyond the condition of workers." (CO, 263)

If as individuals we have kept ourselves from drawing sustenance from our social environment, and if the structures of our society have proved a hindrance to drawing life from our surroundings, then what are the possibilities for remedying uprootedness? Weil saw a partial solution in redressing certain imbalances within the society, such as ridding ourselves of any ultimate emphasis on money and redesigning the conditions of labor so as to make them less oppressive. However, she also recognized that more radical solutions were also required—solutions that would understand society as a vital element in our spiritual life. At least three of the solutions Weil proposes are relevant to us. The first is the most theoretical; it demands a rethinking of how we ought to deal with our neighbors. The second and third solutions, which have to do with education and labor, are means by which she thinks we can grow roots.

The Need for Roots is a book that represents Weil's attempt to analyze the moral bases of society. It is a prime example of how far Weil's theological and social sensibilities have interpenetrated: her "mysticism" is brought to bear upon the difficult, concrete problems of social life, while her sense of social justice is used to serve an ultimate transcendent purpose. At the beginning of *The Need for Roots* she starts her analysis by challenging a commonly accepted idea, namely, that "rights" is the fundamental moral category we should use in dealing with our neighbors and that "rights" provide the moral basis of society. Instead of rights, she claims, we ought to recognize that the notion of *obligations* is primary; what we owe to others is morally prior to any rights that we might demand for ourselves. By contending for the primacy of obligations, Weil seems to strike a chord in our deepest moral sensibility. We give our highest praise to those people who act out of an inner moral sense to others, and whenever we hear people clamoring for their "rights" we suspect something less than altruism is at work. When we clamor for our rights, we seem to place ourselves at the center of the moral universe. As Weil writes: "To place the notion of rights at the center of social conflicts is to inhibit any possible impulse of charity on both sides." (SE, 21) When she adds that our demand for rights is always made in a tone of contention, we feel that she has put her finger on a fundamental and important distinction. It would seem that a just society is one in which people see their first duty as one of caring for the needs of others.

Weil is not done, however. She goes on to say that obligations are not simply a matter of social morality; instead, they are rooted in the transcendent. Obligations alone, she states, "belong to a realm situated above all conditions, because it is situated above this world." (NR, 4) Because they are transcendent, obligations are universal and not an accident of any culture. But why are obligations rooted in the transcendent? It is, Weil thinks, because first and foremost they treat the real inner needs of people. The person who recognizes her obligations to another is one who recognizes that the person with whom she is dealing is sacred and needs to be treated as such. When we base our morality on rights, however, the sacredness of other people is in a practical way not always apparent; we can easily play our own rights off against theirs. When obligations are primary, however, we must always think of others first. Ironically, it is by respecting others that we do ourselves the most good, for then we are acting as people who are also sacred. Thus the very possibility of realizing our own worth in the eyes of God consists in our respecting the worth of others. We are made good by doing good, and doing good means paying attention to our neighbors. It is only because of the grace implicit in attention that we can hope to find our own good without making of our neighbors an object and an opportunity for our own self-aggrandizement.

It is by making obligations the core of social morality that Weil actually puts social morality on a transcendent footing, and makes it a matter of grave spiritual concern. We can see this in the twofold base of obligations. On the one hand, the transcendent nature of obligations consists in the fact that we find our own worth in the eyes of God when we care for others. On the other hand, it also consists in the fact that others also have a worth in the eyes of God that commands our respect. All human beings alike, Weil says, have a spiritual destiny prepared for them by God, and this destiny must be respected. Yet there appears to be a problem here—how can I, a limited and finite creature, meet what amounts to an infinite need on the part of my neighbor? How can I actually respect her sacredness in a meaningful way?

We cannot in the final analysis provide for the ultimate spiritual needs of any human being; that is left to God alone. We can, however, provide the earthly things that are necessary to sustain life while our spiritual needs are being fulfilled by God. We can provide a physical, moral and spiritual environment that allows others to draw life from their surroundings and which helps them avoid seeing life as oppressive and without purpose. It is in this way that we can pay respect to others. Weil notes that there are numerous needs the human being has in order to sustain life.

There are physical needs that can be assuaged by food, shelter, and medical care. A person who does not receive these things may feel the cold and brutal shock of the universe in such a way that he becomes paralyzed and incapable of contemplating any purpose beyond providing for himself. It is therefore an obligation for us to provide these things for others. Yet needs are not only physical—for, as Weil adds, there are also needs of the soul, which are analogous to the body's needs for food. If these latter needs are not being met, the heart can easily shrivel and die.

It is not possible for us to satisfy all these needs by ourselves; as Weil lists what some of them might be it becomes apparent that such needs can only be met through society. Among them she includes, in antithetical pairs, such things as liberty-obedience, equality-hierarchism, responsibility-initiative, honor-punishment, truth-freedom of opinion, security-risk, and private property-collective property. The degree to which a society can balance these needs, and not just oscillate between the members of the pairs, she writes, is the degree to which it succeeds in providing spiritual nourishment for its members.

It should be clear from Weil's list that she considers the existence of a social collective in itself a matter of great importance. Not only do many of these needs of the soul arise because we live in societies, many of them can be balanced only within a societal framework. For example, the need to have property to call my own is hard to reconcile with my need to share in property owned in common with my neighbors. In a nation, however, both kinds of ownership can occur. Society, in this case, becomes an extremely important element in our lives in terms both of what we need from it and of how we are to use it in order to give to others. Understood in this vein, though, it is clear that the importance of society consists in its ability to support and nourish the lives under its care, and not as an entity important in itself.

Because the social sphere is meant to nourish human life and worth, however, it must, in turn, also command some degree of respect from us. If we do not respect the common life, as we do when we neglect it or deliberately undermine it, then we can ultimately destroy the support it gives to others. In effect, by undermining a society we are harming others whom we ought to respect. Weil writes: "We owe respect to a collectivity, of whatever kind—country, family or any other—not for itself but because it is food for a certain number of human souls." (NR, 7) It is therefore an obligation to respect a social collectivity, because by doing so we respect the people who live in it.

Weil believed that if a collectivity is truly based on obligations to others, and if its members act out of respect for others, then it can mediate the divine in some very important ways. In the first place, the social body provides support for all who participate in it. While simply participating in a society does not mean we have found a direct link to God, nevertheless it is through the notion of the common good that we first learn a sense of morality, justice and the idea of God. If we never learned a sense of justice or the idea of God, we would have no starting-point from which to progress in order to find further connections to God. It is for this reason that Weil further argues that it is necessary to construct social relations in a way that makes it possible for us to see further links.

In the second place, a society can also function as a bridge to God for those who contribute to its welfare and thus to the welfare of the people who live in it. Insofar as we give our respect to the society and its members, we are renouncing our own self-centered perspective in order to serve others. When we live as part of a society we have an obligation to suspend our own selfish desires for the life of the whole, and when we do so we ultimately discover a sacrificial love.

There is, of course, a definite sense in which Weil is being a utopian when she suggests that we reconstitute society on the basis of obligations to others, and in such a way that it will function as a link to our spiritual destiny. It is difficult for us to imagine political leaders actually trying to make of these ideas the basis of a concrete platform for action, or using them for anything beyond political rhetoric, although this may reflect more on politicians than on Weil's ideas. Nevertheless, Weil is not foolishly naive in what she suggests. Although she might not have expected

The Love of God in Daily Life

that an entire national constitution would be reformed strictly along her principles, there is a value in making these suggestions. The value is that they provide a standard by which to measure the worth of a society.

A society that strives to meet the inner and outer needs of people and encourages its members to satisfy the needs of others is one that contributes to spiritual well-being. By contrast, any society that shirks meeting the needs of the human soul or hinders us from acting on obligations, such as when it institutes tax laws that make it easier to be acquisitive than to come to the aid of others, contributes to uprootedness and to an ultimate sense of meaninglessness. In addition, Weil suggests a further use we can make of societies. Unless a society is absolutely destitute of spiritual value, we can learn to see what role it might come to play in spirituality. We can, for example, use what fairness that exists already in the society to develop a deeper sense of justice, and we can use its structures to aid others.

The basis of a correct use of social structures begins in recognizing our obligations to others. This is how we begin to grow roots. Weil also adds a number of concrete proposals which she believes, if enacted, would also help a society to become more rooted. Since many of them belong to her native France, they need not concern us here. There are two proposals, however, that do. These concern education and the place of labor within a society, and they have to do with the means by which roots are grown in every generation and in every place.

Education has always been of prime importance in helping individuals to find roots in their culture. Because education forms the character of the members of a society, who in turn determine the culture, it is also a prime mark of the quality of a culture. We perhaps do not see this latter point, since our education has become increasingly technical and professional and we tend to view it as one more tool to do a job. Weil did not see it this way at all. Like the ancient Greeks, whose word for education—*paideia*—means not only "child-rearing" but also "culture," including its moral aspects, Weil saw education as having a strong moral importance. Education for her is not merely a matter of presenting the facts about our existence; it is also the light and perspective in which these facts are presented. Weil understood well the insight of contemporary philosophy and historiography that there is no such thing as a pure "objective" fact. Everything that we call a fact is colored by interpretation, an interpretation that includes a sense of value. Therefore whenever we use facts to make or support judgments, we stand on a system of values as much as on what is "really the case."

One of Weil's favorite examples of this moral coloring of facts is found in the way we write history. As historians know, we cannot escape choosing and highlighting certain facts and not others when we write about a historical topic. We choose these facts because *we* judge them important. To give one example, it remains a perpetual enigma to history whether Napoleon was a great liberator of Europe or a power-mad conqueror; he has been seen both ways by his contemporaries and by moderns. Judging whether he was one or the other should depend on the facts, yet the facts we choose and the way we portray them very much depends upon our possessing certain political and ethical values. The selection of certain facts and our coloring of them is unavoidable, and it does not destroy the enterprise of writing history. Weil adds, however, that this sense of what constitutes importance has behind it a not-so-subtle sense of what we think is truly great and what is not. In teaching history, for example, a professor who believed that greatness lay in strength and not in wisdom might hold the Roman Empire up as a model. This would be giving an interpretation, a moral coloring, to the facts. What is interesting here is not that such a view suppresses knowledge of the cruelty of the Romans, since it doesn't, but that Rome could be held up as a model of greatness at all—and therefore something to be emulated. Countless regimes have compared themselves to Rome and because of this many undesirable features of Rome have been emulated. We also tend to the illusory belief that true greatness can be achieved by methods that are less than great. As Weil writes: "The love of the good will never spring up in the hearts of the population in general,

The Love of God in Daily Life

so long as people believe that in no matter what sphere greatness can be the result of something other than the good." (NR, 237)

It is because she believes that teaching does and should have moral impact that Weil thinks that *all* teaching should contain an explicit evaluation of its subject matter in relation to a goodness that is permanent and universal. Short-sighted nationalism, for example, which compares the best in one nation to the worst in others, is to be avoided at all costs. Instead we must compare everything to the highest possible standard. It is only when everybody sees what they are doing in the light of the good itself that a people and their leaders can ever be expected to build a truly nourishing society.

When Weil says that all teaching must be done in the light of a permanent and universal good, she means that literally. Not even the sciences are exempt from this requirement. In fact, she even goes so far as to say that the sciences (actually, the scientists) that have claimed a neutrality for science and said that questions of value have no place, do a great deal to foster the belief that there is no permanent and universal good. Thus they have contributed to the phenomenon of uprootedness. Such scientists do not always see their endeavors as links to a higher truth, and often reject the notion that there is a higher truth to which science might lead. Many scientists, of course, do not deny that there is a higher truth than science. However a problem arises when science is claimed to be neutral and totally objective within its own realm, and yet at the same time enjoys a popular authority. People then come to believe that there are areas of thought and action that do not have anything to do with a higher truth. If, however, there is a higher truth and a universal good, then science is no more exempt from being evaluated on those terms than ethics or history.

I do not think that by this argument Weil intended that students should begin to discuss the social merits of arithmetic equations, nor that every subfield and experiment must have immediate application to a religious metaphysics. What she does mean is that scientists must step back from their investigations at some point in order to ask what their discoveries tell us about the workings of God's providence—for, Weil says, the necessary laws of the world's interactions that they study *is* God's providence. If scientists fail to do this, then either they are producing a truncated science or else their motives for doing science are other than those of attempting to understand the world. Their motivation is, perhaps, the technological manipulation of the world or the gaining of prestige in a very prestigious field. In either case they are motivated by gravity itself, not by a desire to understand gravity.

Science is not theology, of course, nor is theology one of the natural sciences. Nor did Weil envision a collapse of the distinctions between the two. What she did see a need for was an effort of translation that would make the truths of one field relevant to another. This translation is not a matter of putting the ideas of one field in terms of the other—this is probably impossible—but of making the insights of the two fields mutually enlightening and helpful in our coming to understand what is truly good.

Translation is a way of making true values apparent as people actually have to live and think them. A teacher who effectively translates, for example, would not simply give the historical facts about Napoleon nor use his life as an object lesson. Instead she would try to get her students to understand how historical contingencies and human actions are interrelated, and how thinking about Napoleon's career and his times still has an impact today. To do this she must not only understand the man and his times, and something about ethical values, but also the present and future needs of her students. Translation, in other words, must not be limited to abstract schemes; it must be a genuine attempt to help us understand true value.

Weil is perhaps her own best example of this sort of teacher when she adapted Greek classical tragedy in a factory newspaper for workers. She understood that the workers felt they had to take oppressive orders within a factory system that did not make sense to them, and this system thwarted any opportunity they might have to act courageously on values that really did affect them. To this end she retold the story of Antigone, who could either obey the orders of the state, headed by her tyrannical uncle, or show her love for her dead brother when her uncle would not allow him to be buried in an honorable way. Weil points out that in choosing to act on her obligation to her brother, Antigone chose her own death. She also points out that, within the story, the uncle faced his own destruction because he had put her to death. At the end of her piece Weil then translates the closing lines of the play this way: "The haughty words of arrogant men are paid for by terrible disasters from which in old age they learn moderation." (IC, 23) Although Weil's retelling of the story was faithful to the original and contained no political overtones beyond those in the play, the factory owner saw it as revolutionary and forbade the publication of any other of her efforts. All that Weil had done was to make the truth of an ancient story accessible to workers—yet perhaps the owner was right in judging that to be revolutionary. In short, the task of translation is not to popularize, which only waters down things that sophisticated people supposedly know, it is the building of bridges between the truth that nourishes the soul and the people who are to be fed by it.

The success of people who, like Weil, can effectively translate is often due to the fact that they pay close attention to our deepest needs and the good that will satisfy them. While such people are always essential in helping us to understand values better, Weil thought that uprootedness in a culture makes it extremely difficult either to be an effective translator or to grasp the translation. Within an uprooted culture different areas of our lives simply do not seem to hang together; all subtlety is lost. What is needed, therefore, is a broad coherence of the various cultural symbols—literary, scientific, philosophical, and religious— by which we experience the world.

Ideally this coherence might be achieved by employing what she calls "a double symbolism." By double symbolism she means the use of a common set of symbols for two different areas of life, and in numerous essays Weil gives examples of how this double symbolism works. Workers who lift and carry heavy loads, for example, might take the cross as a symbol. On the one hand the cross can be thought of as a balance, and balances are important in the carrying of loads. On the other hand, the cross has its own religious significance. Therefore, workers who carry loads and use balances might see the relevance of their work to their spiritual life and *vice versa*.

Similarly, Weil contends that farmers and agricultural laborers ought to be made aware of the agricultural parables in the gospels, and such passages ought to play a prominent role in the liturgies of rural areas. To do this is not to make God in our own image; it is, instead, to allow us to see how what we do in daily life actually plays an important role within God's creation as a whole and to see how God's love for us is manifest in our daily lives. Thus, for example, not only would a farmer who repeatedly hears the passage "... unless a seed fall in the ground and die ..." be able to relate his own situation to what is being said and understand the passage better, he would find increased significance in his daily labor. Each time he planted a seed he might have cause to reflect on this passage and its meaning. This would give his vocation a link to God.

Yet we are not saved by symbols themselves, even if they are mutually enlightening. We are only helped by them insofar as we become able to participate in life more fully through them. In this sense, to be effective, symbols must not be *descriptions* of roots or of intellectual constructs, but rather be representative of the ways we can and do actually draw spiritual life from the world around us. We cannot invent this double symbolism; instead we must discover it for ourselves in the ways that our thoughts and activities cohere, and draw upon it in order to give a sense of coherence to life. Symbols must, therefore be drawn from our daily life, both to enlighten it and to indicate the direction our spiritual progress must take.

From where, then, in daily life are spiritual symbols to be drawn? After all, we do many different things in the course of the day and not every thing we do is particularly laudable or worthy of further thought. For Weil, the answer is that our spiritual symbols should be drawn from our daily labor, particularly physical labor, such as she has already suggested in the

The Love of God in Daily Life

case of farmers and workers who carry heavy loads. If they are drawn from this area of life, such symbols would illumine our most basic activities.

Weil has a very specific reason why spiritual symbols should be related to labor, and it has to do with what is for Weil the intrinsic spiritual significance of labor itself—a significance that even the Greeks failed to see. When we freely consent to labor, we also consent to the necessity which rules the world as God's providence. It is a recognition that we are not creatures of unlimited power and that we are not self-sufficient, that we must rely on others and upon the creation itself to live. Ultimately this means that we must recognize our dependence on God for our life; thus, for Weil, labor is a consent to God's will. It is a consent to be the sort of creatures he made us. Weil develops this idea of labor as consent to God's will in an ingenious interpretation of the curse laid upon Adam for his original disobedience in the garden. Adam, she points out, is condemned to labor and death as his punishment. God, however, in passing this sentence is not attempting to exact vengeance on Adam nor does he actually curse him. Rather, because he is just, God chooses a punishment that will reconcile human beings to God and restore them. Thus "labor and death, if man undergoes them in a spirit of willingness, constitute a transference back into the current of supreme Good, which is obedience to God." (NR, 300)

Adam's consent to death and labor as a surrender to God's will is in a way parallel to the consent to affliction. It is a consent to be the same "nothingness" that God originally brought into being. But by a paradoxical turn, to agree to this death is also to agree to draw *all* our life from God. To consent thus is to have full life, for it means giving into God's hands everything that we are.

Death, however, is faced only once in life; affliction may come only to a few. Both affliction and death are also a final and complete wrenching away of the inner person from all that the world has made of it. This wrenching away, Weil thinks, permits us to be spiritually naked and allows us to be brought into God's presence explicitly. But there are also milder ways of accomplishing the same thing, ways to which we can become accustomed and which also prepare us for an ultimate act of consent. The consent to perform labor is one of these ways—to consent to labor, Weil says, is to consent to "a daily death." Weil is not being a nihilist, but rather is pointing out that consent to labor is agreeing to be what God makes of us. This is how we consent to his will. Each day's labor becomes a renewed opportunity for that consent, and through daily practice the ability to consent to actual death or affliction is not an impossibility for those who have undergone such preparation.

It is for these reasons that labor needs to be at the spiritual core of any society. The true and full life of human beings derives from a consent to God's life-giving will, even if that will at times appears to operate in ways contrary to our expectations. True life depends on the presence of God's goodness, and in our daily lives we touch that good most completely through our labor. In labor all our being is engaged, our minds and our bodies; it is a submission to God's will expressed in the providence of the world. To denigrate labor is to cut off a most valuable source of good. But it also becomes apparent that in order for a society to become a source of nourishment for its citizens, it must honor labor and seek by every means possible to make its value apparent to all who perform it. In this way both the society and the daily labors performed within it can mediate the life of human beings and the love of God who created them. Both labor and social life can thus become clear links to the love of God. Furthermore, they become important stages of spiritual progress by which we prepare ourselves for a full and direct contact with God. If we should ever be visited by affliction, the spiritual progress we have made would help prepare us to consent to it and to find in it an opportunity to give back all to God's love.

Weil's writings on the value of labor at the end of *The Need for Roots* are among the last words she wrote. They do not, however, trail off; instead, they bring her ideas around full circle. Whereas she began to discover the reality of God and his love when she was suffering and confused after her discovery of affliction in the factories, she now has found a way of uncovering

The Love of God in Daily Life

in labor a spiritual value that she had perhaps only barely suspected in 1934-35. Within the intervening time Weil covered a lot of ground. She had, for instance, to learn what value affliction might have and how God's love can permeate every aspect of our lives, even the social. However, in covering that ground she did not lose the lesson she had learned about suffering. Instead of ignoring the irreducible fact of affliction or trying to avoid it, or perversely suggesting that it alone gives us access to God, she made affliction and the love of God as shown in Christ's cross the focal point of spirituality. With that as a focal point, she could then discover that if we live life with the spirit of sacrifice that was perfected by Christ in affliction, we can, in fact, find and live God's love in all we do. We can think it in our science, we can live it in our society and we can submit to it in our labors. It is with this idea of the universality of God's love that Simone Weil has said something profoundly important to us today.

EPILOGUE

"The extreme greatness of Christianity lies in the fact that it does not seek a supernatural remedy for suffering, but a supernatural use for it."

Gravity and Grace

Suffering, particularly the suffering of people who do not seem to deserve it, has almost always appeared to us as a problem. This is to say that we regard suffering as an aberration in the creation, something that really does not belong to it. Every generation has spawned a massive literature trying to explain the problem of suffering. The explanations have ranged from the sophisticated to the superstitious, yet the vast majority of them have the common feature of seeing suffering as a problem to be explained or solved.

The extreme importance of Simone Weil lies in the way she challenges this assumption about suffering. Far from being an aberration, suffering is as much a part of the reality of creation as our own existence. Certainly the existence of suffering is as much a mystery as the existence of creation, but it is nevertheless a fact. We are creatures who live by exercising force, but we are also subject to force and often we are its victims. We cannot have one without the other, although we do not often recognize this. In fact, as Weil points out, we go to great lengths to avoid recognizing this. Yet, as she adds, the recognition really constitutes the key to understanding the reality of our lives. Suffering by itself does not wholly constitute our lives, but it is one part of them and unless we recognize that, we run the risk of misunderstanding the whole.

Weil's idea that suffering constitutes a key to understanding life, and that it is not an insuperable obstacle to life, has a number of bases. The first is her belief that we ignore suffering. We are not ignorant of suffering in the sense that we do not know it occurs, for we do, but we are ignorant to the degree that we do not consider it as much of a possibility for us until it happens. So we are often genuinely surprised when we suffer. In this case our ignorance of suffering is rather like a physicist who tries to do an experiment but constantly avoids including the unavoidable variable that, in fact, is a crucial part of the formula he is trying to write from the experiment. We think of suffering as something that keeps upsetting our experiments; Weil, however, thinks it is such an important part of them that without it we cannot reach any true understanding of life. If Weil often seems obsessed with suffering, it is in good part because she wants to draw our attention to suffering when she knows we would rather turn our heads. Our turning away is a problem. It leaves us obdurately convinced that the world is a certain way, merely because we think it ought to be that way; yet we have ignored a great deal of evidence about it. In consequence we continually run the risk of misunderstanding.

For example, we usually live from day to day with certain expectations of life. In fact it is difficult to see how we could do otherwise, since our expectations give shape and meaning to whatever we set out to do. A problem arises, however, when these expectations cease being plans and become the projection of our own limited vision onto the world. It is a problem because then we do not try to see anything beyond ourselves. If we have the power to influence events it is even more of a problem, because we then attempt to make the world fit that vision, accepting as good only what corresponds to that vision and rejecting as evil and unwanted whatever does not. Therefore we limit what we will appreciate, and, in time, we make for ourselves a very limited life, although we might think we have a full one.

A concrete example of how this refusal to accept suffering as a key to understanding a good and a purpose beyond our own expectations comes from a medical ethics case in Indianapolis. A child was born there to a young couple but, unfortunately, the child had Down's Syndrome. As with many Down's Syndrome children, there were life-threatening deformations in her throat and heart; however, both were surgically correctable. The parents, nevertheless, refused the surgery and even went so far as to deny the child nutrition and additional oxygen; the child, of course, died. Aside from the ethical issue involved in denying basic necessities such as food and oxygen, the case presents another moral question, namely, the question of what we will deem acceptable in life. Despite the fact that Down's Syndrome children, particularly if one begins working with them early enough, are often educable and are generally very loving children, apparently the parents would not accept this child as a legitimate human being. In short, it appears that they were only willing to accept life as it is lived on one level, that of middle class people with average or above-average intelligence and looks. Undoubtedly if they had accepted this child they would have had to change their expectations of how life can and should be lived. That is, however, not necessarily a bad thing and many people who have made that change find that there is more goodness and beauty in life than they previously suspected.

Suffering is important to spiritual life because if we are willing to accept it, it allows us to see goodness where we had least anticipated it. We do not have to welcome suffering, but neither can we reject it as unreal. Suffering, Weil thinks, can at least be a way of opening a door to our understanding of a good that exists in the world beyond our expectations. Suffering by itself, however, does not automatically open this door. That door is only opened, Weil adds, if, in suffering, we consent to sacrifice our expectations and wait for that good. In this sense, Weil is not only concerned with suffering but also with our attitude towards it. Unless we are willing to sacrifice our efforts to maintain a position at the center of the universe, we will only experience suffering as a pain with no redeeming qualities.

Weil has still another reason for insisting on suffering and sacrifice as a key to reality, and that is her belief that the world itself is created and redeemed by God's own sacrifice and suffering. Although her idea of creation as being a renunciation and a sacrifice on the part of God is an admirable extension of the central importance of Christ's cross in Christianity, she is only one of perhaps a handful of thinkers who have attempted to make the connection explicit. The reason she is among their number is something other than an attempt at mere theological consistency; it is also her concern with showing how skewed our attempts to find value have been whenever we have used force and domination as central metaphors in spirituality. Often it is not even apparent to us that we have given force and domination a privileged status. For example, whenever we try to come to grips with the problem of oppression, we think that the solution lies in giving additional power to the oppressed. Yet Weil would argue that this is by no means the necessary solution. Perhaps it is the worst one of all, because it does not change the way we solve our problems; it only invites others to solve them in the same way that we have tried to do. On the contrary, Weil would argue, the sacrifice that renounces the use of power as a solution may be the only way any true and lasting change may be effected. Therefore when Weil extends her insights about Christ's cross to embrace all of creation, she does it because the cross reveals a fundamental truth about our condition and a way of finding what is truly good.

The importance of Weil's idea of sacrifice is illustrated by the Nobel prize winner Czeslaw Milosz's essay, "The Importance of Simone Weil." There Milosz suggests that the recent decades have been marked not by a moral laxity, but a moral frenzy. I think if we look carefully we can see his point: revolutions, race riots, overt antagonism between the sexes, ideological conflicts between capitalism and Marxism, and even political terrorism are the result of somebody's or some group's moral frenzy. Ironically, we are fighting for morality and for the sake of establishing moral purpose over against the domination of nature. At the same time, however, whenever we are not actively involved in such struggles it is quite apparent that the question of what constitutes morality and purpose is more confused than ever. Weil, Milosz argues, is one of the few people of our age who has tried to think this situation through to the bitter end. After thinking it through she concludes that we are not masters over nature or even our own history; instead, as she argued in her essay on the *Iliad*, we seem to be driven by a blind necessity. The more we struggle against this necessity and believe we are not its subjects, the more we seem to become dominated by it. Despite the fact that we are morally frenzied, our solutions have inevitably been the sort we have always resorted to—that is, ones involving force.

Epilogue

It is to this sort of situation that Weil ultimately addresses herself. Suffering and sacrifice are for her not the esoteric religious practices of "passion mysticism"; they are, instead, the alternatives to force and domination both in personal and social life. In this regard they are an attempt to find life, not a denial of life. We find it difficult to accept this, for if we do, it means a reversal of many of the values we have held dear. It means we are thrust into a void where we have little idea of what we will find to replace them. Yet at the same time that we find ourselves anxious about this untried way, we might well remember the anxiety and fearful dread into which our attempts to dominate nature and peoples have thrust us. We have struggled hard to find some kind of permanent value and peace—we are now sceptical about their possibilities.

Although the use of force and domination has not given us any sense of ultimate purpose and value, sacrifice and its willingness to sacrifice for the life of others might. Weil's life, even in some of its most bizarre aspects, is a witness to that possibility. Her writings show how with the acceptance of suffering and with a willingness to sacrifice all and wait for God, good and purpose might be revealed. It is through sacrifice, Weil says, that we can honor and respect those who do suffer; by that sacrifice we share our lives with them, instead of regarding them as unworthy. It is by sacrifice that we also respect the sacredness of the creation. When we accept it as it is, instead of something to be dominated, we acknowledge that it has its own life, a life that God found good when he created it. Ultimately sacrifice leads us to accept God's will and God's life as our own, and in that we find true life.

NOTES

1. This story of Weil's baptism *in extremis* was first printed in the Jewish journal, *Les Nouveaux Cahiers* in the autumn of 1971 by Wladimir Rabi. It was subsequently retold in Simone Petrement's biography with a difference in the date of the baptism. In May, 1981 I spoke with the person who performed the baptism and am convinced of the truth of the story. The detailed evidence has been presented in a paper delivered to the American Weil Society in May, 1984.

2. Susan Sontag, "Simone Weil" in *Against Interpretation* (New York: Farrar, Straus & Giroux, 1961), p. 50.

3. Ann Loades, "Sacrifice: A Problem for Theology" in *Images of Belief*, ed. David Jaspers (New York: St. Martin's Press, 1984).

4. G. Thibon and J.M. Perrin, *Simone Weil as We Knew Her*, trans. Emma Crauford (London: Routledge & Kegan Paul, 1953), p. 138.

5. *The Revelations of Divine Love of Julian of Norwich*, (St. Meinrad, IN: Abbey Press, 1975), p. 48.

6. *Newsweek* (Dec. 31, 1984), p. 24.

BIBLIOGRAPHY

I. The following is a bibliography of Weil's works in English preceded by their abbreviations used in the text. Works of Weil in French are only cited here if they have been used in the text.

CO	*La Condition ouvriére*. Paris: Gallimard, 1951.
EL	*Ecrits de Londres*. Paris: Gallimard, 1957.
FLN	*First and Last Notebooks*. London: Oxford University Press, 1970.
GW	*Gateway to God*. Glasgow: Collins, 1974.
GG	*Gravity and Grace*. London: Routledge & Paul, 1972.
IC	*Intimations of Christianity among the Ancient Greeks*. London: Routledge & Paul, 1976.
LP	*Lectures on Philosophy*. Cambridge, Cambridge University Press, 1978.
LR	*Letter to a Priest*. New York: Putnam's, 1959.
NR	*The Need for Roots*. New York: Harper & Row, 1976.
NB	*The Notebooks of Simone Weil*. 2 volumes, London: Routledge & Paul, 1956.
OL	*Oppression and Liberty*. Amherst: University of Massachusetts Press, 1973.
SN	*On Science, Necessity and the Love of God*. London: Oxford, University Press, 1968.
SE	*Selected Essays, 1934-1943*. London: Oxford University Press, 1962.
SL	*Seventy Letters*. London: Oxford University Press, 1965.
SWR	*The Simone Weil Reader*. New York: David McKay, 1977.
WG	*Waiting for God*. New York: Harper & Row, 1973.

Bibliography

II. Other works of Weil:

Formative Writings: 1929–1941. Edited by D. McFarland and W. Van Ness. New York: Routledge & Paul, 1987.
Oeuvres complètes. Sixteen volumes. Paris, Gallimard, 1988–.
Oeuvres. Paris, Gallimard, 1999.
Simone Weil. Edited by E. Springsted. Maryknoll, NY: Orbis, 1998.
Simone Weil: An Anthology. Edited by S. Miles. New York: Grove, 2000.
Simone Weil on Colonialism—An Ethic of the Other. Edited by J. P. Little. Lanham, MD: Rowman & Littlefield, 2003.
War and the Iliad. New York: New York Review of Books Classics, 2005.

III. The following is a select bibliography of secondary works on Weil in English that may be helpful to the reader.

Allen, D. and E. Springsted. *Spirit, Nature and Community: Issues in the Thought of Simone Weil.* Albany: State University of New York Press, 1994.
Allen, D. *Three Outsiders.* Cambridge: Cowley, 1983.
Avery, D. *Beyond Power: Simone Weil and the Notion of Authority.* Lanham, MD: Lexington, 2008.
Bell, Richard. *Simone Weil—The Way of Justice as Compassion.* Lanham, MD: Rowman & Littlefield, 1998.
———, editor. *Simone Weil's Philosophy of Culture.* Cambridge: Cambridge University Press, 1993.
Blum, L., and V. Seidler. *A Truer Liberty—Simone Weil and Marxism.* London: Routledge, 1989.
Cabaud, J. *Simone Weil: A Fellowship in Love.* New York: Channel, 1964.
Coles, R. *Simone Weil—A Modern Pilgrimage.* Reading, MA: Addison-Wesley, 1987.
Dargan, J. *Simone Weil: Thinking Poetically.* Albany: State University of New York Press, 1999.
Deitz, M. *Between the Human and the Divine: The Political Thought of Simone Weil.* Totowa, NJ: Rowman & Littlefield, 1988.
Doering, J., and E. Springsted, editors. *The Christian Platonism of Simone Weil.* Notre Dame: University of Notre Dame Press, 2004.

Bibliography

Dunaway, J., and E. Springsted. *The Beauty that Saves: Essays on Aesthetics and Language in Simone Weil.* Macon, GA: Mercer University Press, 1996.

Finch, H. L. *Simone Weil and the Intellect of Grace.* New York: Continuum, 1999.

Little, J. P. *Simone Weil: Waiting on Truth.* Oxford: Berg, 1988.

McClellan, D. *Simone Weil: Utopian Pessimist.* London: Macmillan, 1989.

Morgan, V. *Weaving the World—Simone Weil on Science, Mathematics and Love.* Notre Dame: University of Notre Dame Press, 2005.

Perrin, J-M., and G. Thibon. *Simone Weil as We Knew Her.* London: Routledge, 2003.

Petrément, S. *Simone Weil: A Life.* New York: Pantheon, 1976.

Rhees, R. *Discussions of Simone Weil.* Albany: State University of New York Press, 2000.

Rozelle-Stone, R., and L. Stone, editors. *Relevance of the Radical: Simone Weil 100 Years Later.* New York: Continuum, 2009.

Springsted, E. *Christus Mediator: Platonic Mediation in the Thought of Simone Weil.* Chico, CA: Scholars, 1983.

Vëto, M. *The Religious Metaphysics of Simone Weil.* Albany, NY: State University of New York Press, 1994.

von der Ruhr, M. *Simone Weil: An Apprenticeship in Attention.* New York: Continuum, 2007.

Winch, P. *Simone Weil The Just Balance.* Cambridge: Cambridge University Press, 1989.

www.ingramcontent.com/pod-product-compliance
Lightning Source LLC
Chambersburg PA
CBHW072149160426
43197CB00012B/2313